VERY
SWEDISH

© Bokförlaget Max Ström 2007

© Text Annica Triberg

© Photo/food Per Ranung

© Photo/nature Tore Hagman

Chef Lena Salomonsson

Graphic design & Styling Victoria Bergmark

Translation Kim Loughran & Lukas Loughran

Language editing and proof-reading Kristiina Sepänmaa

Lithograhy & printing Fälth & Hässler, Värnamo

ISBN 978-91-7126-099-4

Annica Triberg Per Ranung Tore Hagman

VERY
SWEDISH

BOKFÖRLAGET MAX STRÖM

Foreword

What shapes a country's gastronomic identity? The answer used to be easy: its plant and animal life. Depending on where you lived, conditions varied for what you could grow, hunt or fish. And since Sweden is so characteristically elongated from north to south, with fertile Skåne in the south and untamed Lapland in the north, we developed different eating habits, perhaps more so than any other country.

Today, whatever ingredients you desire can be found anywhere in the country, so people in the extreme north are as happy with their pizza as the folks in the south are with their Thai food. But some dishes seem to be part of our Swedish DNA: strawberry layer cake at Midsummer, pickled herring at Christmas and cinnamon rolls with coffee. Not to mention meatballs with lingonberry preserve!

This is a legacy to cherish. There are tastes that exist only here, ingredients that only we cook the way we do. True, almost every culture has a version of *pyttipanna*, whether it's called paella or nasi goring. Others make *kåldolmar*, the meat-and-rice mix wrapped in leaves, and even more have their own meatballs. But never exactly like ours. Sometimes we Swedes put ourselves down, believing that only the food made by star chefs is worth shouting about. But we have a long country embellished with delicacies. Let's be like southern Europeans: the French eat French food, the Italians eat Italian and in Greece it's Greek food. And, seeing that national pride, others want first to sample, then cook the recipes. Which is the reason for this book on Swedish food.

A look at Swedish geography will show 25 provinces, from Skåne in the south to Lapland in the north. The provinces' borders gradually took shape during the 1200s and 1300s as natural boundaries for language and traditions of justice.

In the 1600s, the counties were created. This was a bureaucratic concept that in many parts splintered the old provinces. But the tradition of provinces survives. And even if Swedish is now spoken throughout the country and we abide by the same code of law, local dialects still exist to a great extent and there is a strong sense that the provinces' different characters are worth nurturing.

When it comes to the differences in eating habits from north to south, boundaries are created not by provincial or county lines but by geography. Proximity to the sea and its coastline, to forest and lake, to highlands and wilderness, or to field and meadow has formed our Swedish gastronomy. So in sorting the recipes into sections for this book, we looked at where the ingredients originate. Mostly, we chose not local specialties but dishes that are nowadays made and served throughout Sweden. Some recipes are traditional, others more recent. Together, they make up a smorgasbord of Swedish flavours. Food we long for.

Annica Triberg

SEA AND COAST

On a summer day on Käringö island on the west coast, the jetty glows orange. It's not colour from an unusually beautiful sunset — it's a dozen youngsters in life vests, lying on their stomachs and excitedly fishing for tiny crabs. The kids are all in a row, lost in time and space. Their existence is a piece of string and a crab scuttling around in the shallow water. Let Dad yell all he wants that it's time to come home to eat; hunger is on hold until the crab is caught.

We leave the kids and find a place to sit high on a rock, warmed by a benign sun. From a basket we extract freshly boiled Norwegian lobsters (langoustines), white bread and a little jar of homemade mayonnaise. The basket is integral; a picnic isn't a picnic without a basket, ideally covered with a chequered cloth. There's our Swedishness again — it's as if we have picnic guidelines programmed into our genes.

The lobsters are still warm, the French bread is crisp and the mayonnaise is heavenly, bulging with egg yolk and oil. Afterwards, following a dip in the sea to cool down as much as for washing our hands after the lobster orgy, we sit still, fingers laced around coffee cups. Our gaze drifts off into the distance beyond the Pater Noster rocks. We accept logically that the world is round. That the sea doesn't suddenly end and that we don't have to follow the Vikings' warning: "If only you sail to the right when you reach Rome, you will not sail off the edge." And yet, looking at an unbroken horizon, you start to wonder. Doesn't it end somewhere?

For a country like Sweden where about two thirds of land area is close to the sea, there are many places where you can contemplate this. As the crow flies, we have 2,700 kilometres of coastline. Measuring each bay and inlet, it would be immensely more. The landscape varies endlessly. From quiet bays disturbed by only the strongest storms, via archipelagos with countless small islands and treacherous rocks, to the open sea where one's smallness is immediately apparent as soon as God sneezes. Swedes often associate archipelagos with the Stockholm one, with its 30,000 islands of various sizes. But there are "flyspecks" on sea charts around most of our coast; only the provinces of Skåne and Halland are without.

The flyspecks metaphor was coined by a visiting Frenchman about ten years ago. He wanted to rent a boat to go sailing with his family for a month. When the boat rental agent handed him his sea chart, the Frenchman brushed absent-mindedly at the plastic sheathing, believing the smallest islands were flyspecks. It ended with the family cruising the Göta Canal under engine power.

"Reality has loosed its moorings," writes author Pär Westberg in a piece about the Swedish coast. The coastline was sculpted largely by inland ice, scraping, grooving

Högby lighthouse on the island of Öland.

The pantry

Herring
Baltic herring
Common whitefish
Salmon
Vendace roe
Potatoes
Eel
Shrimps
Crab
Norway lobster
Lobster

and polishing the rocks as it retreated, leaving all manner of odd formations. Thanks to the Gulf Stream, Sweden's waters are warm (everything is relative), allowing fish and flora to flourish, even if we humans have done our best over the years to deplete fish stocks and push back plant growth to make room for the urban dream.

Let's start in the north. We begin by following a fishing boat out of Kalix in Norrbotten province. It's after the small vendace, and especially its roe (sometimes incorrectly called bleak roe which is from another sort of fish), that gold from the sea sold in tiny jars and with a flavour even Russian caviar cannot match. On Storön island off Kalix, several tonnes of vendace roe are produced every year. One of its great advantages is that it can be deep-frozen and re-frozen. Take out the jar, thaw it enough to scrape out what you need, then replace in the freezer. Serve the roe on bread fried in butter with chopped red onion, sour cream and a lemon wedge.

For a long time, Norrbotten was populated only along its Baltic coastline, since the sea was the main food source. Later, people moved inland. They followed the mighty rivers and met with Sami people and in the north along the Torne river Finnish language and customs also joined the broth. The Torne Valley was populated early, thanks to the fish in the Torne River. An annual common whitefish festival at the Kukkolaforsen rapids attracts numbers of visitors to fish the swift waters or just to enjoy fresh common whitefish along the banks. It is good salt-cured, hot-smoked, cold-smoked or simply grilled over an open fire. Another speciality from Norrbotten is the Arctic char: lightly salted and baked it's a true joy.

The city of Piteå has lent its name to *pitepalt,* a famous savoury dumpling made from grated raw potato, barley flour and milk and served with clarified butter and often pan-fried salted pork. *Paltbröd* is a bread baked from rye flour and blood. The main liquid ingredient is sometimes *svagdricka,* a malt drink with low alcohol content. The bread is baked and then dried. Before being served it is boiled in salty water. Before freezers, drying bread was a good way of preserving it.

Västerbotten (väst = west) province is south of Norrbotten (norr = north), despite what the name implies. Österbotten (öst = east) is in Finland, and Söderbotten (söder = south) doesn't even exist. Postglacial land rise is obvious in Västerbotten.

The coastal people fished but also sawed timber at river mills and burned tar. Huge power stations on Sweden's wide and strong northern rivers provide us with hydropower but one major river is untouched: the Vindelälven, now a mecca for anglers with images of perch, grayling and salmon trout glistening in their eyes. Salmon has been a staple along the coast. It is served cold-poached or in soup with barley grain and root vegetables. You can eat it in a softbread wrap called a "squeeze" (*klämma*). The modern *klämma* can also be built around smoked reindeer meat or a wedge of Västerbotten cheese.

Västerbotten cheese, or "Vasterbotten" as it's often spelt, is a gourmet favourite, and our gratitude goes to the originator, Eleonora Lindström, who worked at a dairy in Västergötland province in the 1860s. One of her colleagues was Leonora Mortensson, immigrated from Schleswig-Holstein. Perhaps their name similarity led Leonora to share her recipes for Swiss cheeses. Eleonora later moved to Västerbotten province and by 1871 had perfected the cheese that is arguably Sweden's most appreciated. Sweden's former caterer to the royal court, Werner Vögeli, himself born in Emmental in Switzerland, was a famous fan.

Another province favourite is the skinny little almond potato, gold-yellow inside and with a rich taste of long, bright summer nights. Reindeer and game are numerous and there has even been sheep farming here. Little of the animal was wasted; the shoulder was salted and dry-smoked over an open fire and called "sheep fiddle" (*fårfiol*) because the shape vaguely suggests a violin. These days, preparation has been modernised but the tender, flavourful meat is still hard to beat. The mutton suet went to a dish that would make today's GI fanatics faint: the suet was fried until crisp and served in a sauce thickened with fat from the pan. (!) This makes the inlanders' smoked and dried reindeer meat a healthier dish — and great as an accompaniment to drinks.

The next two provinces to the south both stink. Whether that's good or bad is purely a matter of taste — Ångermanland and Medelpad lead Sweden in their love for *surströmming*, fermented herring. The best-known cannery was on the island of Ulvön in a fishing village that dated back to the 1500s. This odd delicacy is encased in bulging cans that look about to burst. Connoisseurs tell you *surströmming* is best enjoyed with thin northern flatbread, sliced almond potatoes, onion and possibly a little goat cheese and a glass of milk. You can also serve it as an oven dish with boiled potatoes on the side. If you're not tempted by fermented fish, there's always fresh Baltic herring, cod and salmon to vary your diet. The lamprey is fished here and often served in soup.

In summer, cattle used to be driven to the outposts where *kams* would be prepared and eaten — it's a savoury dumpling made of milk, soft whey cheese and barley grain and often filled with pork. These days it's mostly made with grated raw potato and barley.

The highlands of Ångermanland stretch to the sea, forming Höga kusten, the "high coast", with its dramatic views, bays, islands and real live fishing villages. This is another part of Sweden listed as a World Heritage by UNESCO. Much of the population lived by, and made use of, the Ångermanälven River. Ådalen Valley was full of sawmills and logs were floated down to the coast and waiting cargo boats.

On their way back south, the boats would pass Medelpad, the forestry industry's fiefdom at the turn of the 20th century, with forestry owners making fortunes from

Left: Vårhallarna, Skåne. Above: Höga kusten, Ångermanland.

the vast woods. They would live it up royally in Sundsvall hotels and stories of drink and food excesses live on in folklore. When downtown Sundsvall's wooden buildings were largely wiped out in a fire at the end of the 1800s the structures erected to replace them were of stone, so the glory town of Swedish forestry is brick and mortar rather than lumber.

The coastline is garnished by fishing villages where salmon catches were periodically so good that it was hard to sell the fish. Farmed salmon are now the norm.

As well as the fruits of the sea, Medelpad's farmers often ate *Norrlandspölsa*, a stew-like dish traditionally made with beef, pork, liver and barley grain, and long a school-canteen horror when made by uninspired cooks. *Tjälknöl* or *tjälknul*, knob of venison, is another traditional northern Swedish dish, cooked long and slow. Whatever the real story of the dish, a modern version involves a woman who tried to thaw frozen venison in the oven and forgot it there overnight, unaware she was using a traditional method. Thinking it ruined and trying to save what could be saved, she put the meat in brine and discovered a new dish.

Another fishing village that used to produce fermented herring, *surströmming*, is Mellanfjärd, on the coast of Hälsingland province. The old storehouse is now a trendy restaurant, with a nostalgic favourite on the drinks list: Pommac, Sweden's fizzy apple pop, which they claim was invented in the province. Hälsingland is rich in forest and water. Logs used to be floated down the Ljusnan River to sawmills by the coast. If you have time for an inland detour, travel to Lassekrog, west of Ljusdal. There's an impressive old forest workers' village with the original, impressive wooden houses intact. If you hear fiddle music on the wind on your way back to the coast, it's probably the annual Hälsinge Hambo festival. It climaxes when thousands of couples in folklore dress dance the highway from Hårga to Järvsö to beautiful, melancholic fiddles and hurdy-gurdies.

Fishing was the backbone of coastal communities and many fishing villages survive, as does traditional cooking. If you're offered *strömmingsklöbb*, it's lightly salted Baltic herring "en croute" and *sotare* is blackened Baltic herring grilled over flames. Several dishes involve *böckling*, smoked Baltic herring: two are *böcklingpudding* (a savoury egg pudding) and *böcklinglåda* (with potatoes).

At Axmar, north of the city of Gävle in Gästrikland province, there's the sea and the bluish slag from the old 17th-century ironworks. Take a seat on the jetty by the bar iron storehouse and think about life in those days. There is more about Gästrikland in the chapter on Forest and Lake.

Next stop is Roslagen, a part of Uppland province where the dramatic coastline of Norrland or northern Sweden gives way to softer shapes and friendly bays. For

Hästvam, Fjällbacka.

years, this was a place much visited by artists and musicians, something of an artist colony. They cherry-picked the bright summer days and left the winter for the locals, eking out a living from fishing.

Poets and painters also frequented the Stockholm archipelago, lending a romantic glow to calloused archipelago hands and thankless tacking against the wind. One poet, Elias Sehlstedt, was less blue-eyed after a period as a customs inspector in Sandhamn, 1852–69. He could be cute, as in "A Little Nest I Want to Build", but when writing about Sandhamn, was grimmer: "...miserable Sandhamn, poor in food and cheer," he wrote. He should see Sandhamn today, an archipelago island with a density of restaurants and celebrities in summer almost like downtown Stockholm's.

We proceed south through the archipelago, passing the upper crust on Dalarö Island and continuing via Utö with its abandoned mines and rich history to Landsort, the archipelago's southernmost satellite. From the old fishing village of Trosa in Södermanland province, where they used to salt Baltic herring and where we now happily dine on it in classy restaurants, we continue to Vikbolandet in Östergötland province. The landscape changes yet again. If luck holds, we'll have a fresh pike-perch from Bråviken bay for dinner tonight.

We make our way south along the coast of Småland province through the Kalmar Sound, turn west at Blekinge province and arrive at Smygehamn in Skåne province. We're as far south as we can get without leaving the country. We write postcards home and post them in Skanör/Falsterbo, threading our way through groups of summer residents in beat-up old bathrobes. (In many old coastal resorts, dress code decrees that the better the family, the more threadbare the beach attire should be.)

Up through Öresund, the sound between Sweden and Denmark, stopping off at the beautiful little island of Ven. Astonishingly, durum wheat, the kind used in Italy's pasta, is grown here. On to Mölle and Kullabygden, where the landscape rises up again with drastic cliffs and steep ravines. Mölle was immortalised in a comic song by Sweden's beloved singing baron, Povel Ramel. In the lyric, a husband is struggling with household chores in town while his wife relaxes by the sea. Perhaps the lady was dining on the famous Mölle plaice, served with Danish-style rémoulade.

Halland province is next, with its summery sandy beaches, especially near Tylösand. Halland has abundant salmon and as early as the Middle Ages, the Nissan River was famous for its fish. They claim even the Pope in Rome had heard about it. This was probably because the Dominican monastery in Halmstad had sole rights to salmon fishing here until the late 1500s. Halland's province dish is salmon pudding with clarified butter — luxury food, you might think, but for years salmon was an everyday staple here. There's even a story that housemaids and stable lads had

Svartlöga in Stockholm archipelago.

the right to demand a certain number of salmon-free meals a week!

On the vegetable side, kale is prized. It's used for soup and at Christmas for *lång-kål* ("long cabbage") in which cream and spices are added to boiled kale. Ideally, kale should be picked after frost, giving it a full-bodied taste. In Halland, the Christmas smorgasbord is incomplete without a big Kvibille cheddar, now popular year-round. Kvibille's cloth covering supposedly originated when an apprentice had to improvise a substitute for cheesecloth when the supply ran out. He cut the arms off a shirt and used those. The Kvibille dairy also makes a tasty blue cheese, Sweden's own Roquefort.

We travel north again, waving to the statue of the fisherman's wife as we pass Gothenburg harbour, and drive to Bohuslän province by way of Hönö and Öckerö islands. Bohuslän is famous for its herring and the shrimps that are sold fresh or smoked in every little harbour-side kiosk. For Swedes, Bohuslän is synonymous with the sea. A third of the province consists of rocks, islands and cliffs. Not very arable, in other words. The sea sustained the people. The local shrimps and Norway lobsters are well known, as are crab and lobster. But the array of shellfish also includes mussels and oysters. Most oysters are from the north of the province where the waters are more salty, and mussels are farmed off Strömstad.

"Get any fish?"

"Nah, only *mackerel*."

That's how it used to be. Some fish were inferior, others, like turbot, superior. Cod and plaice were also among the elite. Today, freshly smoked mackerel is a real gourmet delight and cod is disappearing.

Despite the wealth of fish, Bohuslän's province dish is a dessert, *äggost* and fruit preserve. The dish dates to the Middle Ages and consists of eggs, sour milk and sugar put into a sculpted form and allowed to drain until as thick as crème caramel. It is still a real party treat.

Deep inlets cut into the landscape and offshore lies a rosary of islands. We buy a big bag of fresh shrimps and leave Marstrand and its fortress for Skärhamn, Mollesund, Grundsund, Lysekil, Hunnebostrand and Fjällbacka, arriving in Grebbestad. At Tanumshede, we detour to look at rock carvings (World Heritage-listed, naturally). We are peeling the last of the shrimps when we get to Strömstad. This is where the Swedish coast ends and becomes Norwegian.

Our final stop is out at the Koster Islands. We borrow a moped. It gets us all the way out to the western side to enjoy the sunset. Out there, the old doubts come creeping:

Maybe you *can* fall off the edge?

Näsudden on the island of Gotland.

Fillet of perch with clarified butter and parsley potatoes

Perch are found in Sweden's plentiful lakes and in the low-saline waters of the Baltic Sea. It is one of the finest Swedish fish. Large perch can be filleted or "trousered" — cut to keep the back intact leaving what looks like a pair of pants. Tricky? Ask someone to show you how and you'll see it's relatively simple. Small fish can be scaled or skinned and fried whole with the spine remaining.

Serves 4

4 generous-size perch fillets
1 dl stoneground rye flour
1 tsp salt
a pinch of freshly ground white pepper
oil and butter for frying

Pat the fillets in the flour, then fry in a mixture of oil and butter. A few minutes on each side. Season with salt and pepper.

Clarified butter

100 g butter

Melt the butter over low heat. Skim off the solids and pour carefully into a small jug, leaving the dregs.

Parsley potatoes

800 g new potatoes
a little clarified butter
1 dl chopped parsley
salt

Boil the potatoes in salted water for 15 minutes. Mix the steaming potatoes with a little clarified butter, parsley and salt.

Gravlax with head waiter sauce or sweet mustard sauce

Gravlax dates from the 1300s. Originally, a "grave" was dug and the fish salted and wrapped in birch-bark, then buried, away from hungry animals. These days we "bury" the salmon in the fridge. Use the middle part of a good-sized and not too skinny salmon. Avoid overkill — in other words, don't use more ingredients than the recipe calls for and don't leave the fish more than 24 hours in the fridge or the result could be dry and hard. The mustard-based "head waiter" sauce is a must.

Serves 8 as a main, 15 as a starter

1 kg salmon fillet with skin (ideally a middle piece)
1 dl sugar
1 tbsp coarsely ground white pepper
0.6 dl iodinized coarse salt, zapped in a blender or pounded in a mortar
3 handfuls of fresh dill

Remove bones with tongs. Mix sugar, salt and pepper and massage into the fillet on both sides.
Chop the dill and spread it on the meat side. Put the salmon in a plastic bag or ziplock and seal. Put the bag on a plate and leave at room temperature for about 2 hours to let the mixture melt. Place in the fridge and leave for 24 hours, turning 3–4 times.
Take out the fish, dry it and scrape off the dill and seasoning. Slice thinly. You can even slice up the salmon skin into strips and sear them quickly in a hot pan. *Gravlax* will keep in the fridge for 4–5 days and can also be deep-frozen.

Head waiter sauce

1 tbsp mild mustard
1 tsp Dijon mustard
1 tbsp sugar
2 tbsp vinegar
1 dl oil
1/2 dl finely chopped dill

See that all ingredients are at room temperature. Mix the mustard, sugar and vinegar. Drizzle in oil while mixing swiftly. Mix in the chopped dill. Set aside in a cool place.

Cold poached char with dill mayonnaise

Char is available either wild or farmed. The fish produces its own aspic when boiled whole with its backbone so you won't need gelatine for the attractive jelly. Boiling time can be reduced if the char is allowed to cool in its own cooking liquor. This also retains all the flavours. The same technique will work for pike, perch and salmon. Increase boiling time for larger fish.

Serves 6 as a starter

1 Arctic char, gutted, about 500 g
4 dl white wine vinegar
2 tbsps salt
6 dl water
1/2 tsp white peppercorns
1 bay leaf
5 whole allspice
1 sliced carrot
a few sprigs of dill

Serve with

1 dl chopped dill
1 1/2 dl mayonnaise
boiled potatoes
1 lemon cut into wedges

Gut and rinse the char. Boil the water with all ingredients except the fish. Put in the fish and bring back to the boil. Cover and poach carefully for 3 minutes. Remove the pot from the heat and let cool.
Mix the dill and mayonnaise. Serve the fish cold with dill mayonnaise, lemon wedges and freshly boiled potatoes.

Pickled herring

Herring used to be Sweden's main staple and in the Middle Ages was valuable in trade with Continental Europe. Pickling was a way of extending its shelf-life. This "One-Two-Three" pickling brine (1 part spirit vinegar, 2 parts sugar, 3 parts water) is a modern simplification invented by Karin Chädström. She was long the queen of cold larder chefs in classic Stockholm restaurants such as Operakällaren, Riche and Källaren Diana.

Serves 8 as a starter

3–4 fillets of salt herring, soaked in water overnight
2 bay leaf
1/2 carrot
1 onion
7 cm leek
1 tsp coarsely ground allspice
1/2 tsp coarsely ground white pepper
1/2 tsp coarsely ground black pepper

Pickling brine

1/2 dl spirit vinegar, 12%
1 dl sugar
1 1/2 dl water

Cut the herring fillets into roughly diagonal dominoes. Cut the carrot lengthwise and slice into thin half-moons. Cut the onion into rings and thinly slice the leek. In a glass jar, alternate herring, vegetables and spices. Heat the vinegar and sugar until the sugar dissolves. Add cold water, making sure the brine is not too warm when you pour it over the herring. See that the brine covers the ingredients. A small plate or dish helps keep the fish submerged. Keep cold for two days before serving. Will last at least a week in the fridge.

Jansson's temptation

The dish is far older than the name. Just who Jansson was is disputed. The currently accepted explanation is that the dish got its name from a hit 1928 film of the same name. A Stockholm hostess wanted to give her gal pals a New Year's treat and borrowed the film title to make her simple casserole fancy.

Serves 4

8 medium-size potatoes
2 small onions
15–20 Swedish anchovies (marinated sprat fillets)
2 dl double cream
2 tbsp breadcrumbs
2 tbsp butter + butter for the dish

Set the oven to 200C/400F/GM6. Grease an ovenproof dish. Peel potatoes and cut into matchsticks. Peel and slice the onion and fry golden brown in 1 tablespoon of butter.
Spread half the potato matchsticks on the bottom of the oven dish. Then the onion and sprat fillets, pressing down. Pour in the sprat jus and cream. Sprinkle generously with breadcrumbs and dot with the tablespoon of butter. Bake for 45–50 minutes until the potato is soft and appealingly golden brown.

Freshwater crayfish

Trapping crayfish in a lake under an August moon — for many Swedes, that's as close as you can get to the national soul. The Swedish court received in 1504 a consignment of crayfish from Lübeck in northern Germany. Previously, Swedes had heeded the Bible's warning that: "whatever has no fins nor scales in the waters, that is an abomination to you" (Leviticus 11:12). But the Swedish court was interested in German customs and was soon enjoying the delicacy, to the point of breeding the crustaceans in castle moats.

The taste of dill is paramount in the dish. Use tongs to lift out the crayfish and display them — putting your fingers into the brine increases their perishability.

Serves 4	1 kg live crayfish
Cooking liquor	1 small onion 2 litres water 1/2 dl coarse salt 1 sugarlump 1 bottle of beer, preferably dark 5–6 sprigs of crown dill
Serve with	crispbread toast Västerbotten cheese or strong cheddar beer, aquavit

Peel the onion and slice. Mix all ingredients except the crayfish in a big pot with a lid. Rinse them in cold water and check that they are still living. Boil the liquid fiercely for 10 minutes. Extract the dill with tongs. Put half of the crayfish into the boiling water, cover and let boil 2–3 minutes. Remove the lid, and as soon as they float to the surface pull out the crayfish with the tongs. Repeat until all are boiled. Remove the pot from the heat, put the crayfish back and let cool. As soon as the liquor is cool, put the pot in the fridge and keep overnight.

You can use the same cooking liquor for deep-frozen crayfish, but let them thaw first, then check their saltiness so you don't add too much salt. Put the crayfish into the liquor as soon as it has cooled. Frozen crayfish have already been boiled and should not be re-heated.

Salmon pudding with clarified butter

Laxpudding is normally based on salt-cured lax. But feel free to use smoked salmon or *gravlax*. Or a mix. A modern addition is tomatoes, which contribute colour and a pleasant tang. If you like your pudding compact, assemble it the day before cooking and store in the fridge under a weight.

Serves 4

200–500 g salt-cured or smoked salmon or gravlax
8–10 boiled potatoes
2 eggs
1 1/2 dl milk
1 1/2 dl double cream
1/2 tsp freshly ground white pepper
1 tsp salt
2 bunches of dill
2 tomatoes

Serve with

100 g butter

Warm oven to 200C/400F/GM6. Peel and slice the potatoes. Whisk eggs, milk and cream, seasoning with white pepper and salt.
Chop the dill and slice the tomatoes. Grease the dish. Layer potato, salmon, dill and tomato, with potato on the bottom and top. Pour in the egg mixture and bake 45–50 minutes. Melt the butter over a low heat and serve alongside.

Pike with horseradish

It's not our most beautiful fish, but there's huge pride in catching your own. If you can't go fishing, buy one and savour its delicacy. If you've ever ordered *quenelles* in France, there's a good chance the main ingredient came from Sweden. Along the east coast, from Stockholm south to Blekinge province, this used to be Christmas fare. It was served whole, often filled with marinated sprats for example.

Serves 4

1 1/2–2 kg whole pike
2 tbsp salt per litre water
juice of 1 lemon

Serve with

fresh horseradish
100 g butter
2 boiled eggs
boiled potatoes

Gut and scale the fish. Fillet it, keeping the skin. Divide the fillets in half. Boil the water with salt and lemon juice. Put in the fish, bring back to the boil, then remove from the heat. Leave under the lid for 5 minutes. Take out the fish, remove the skin and serve with clarified butter, chopped egg, grated horseradish and boiled potatoes.

Salt-cured salmon and stewed potatoes with dill

Gravlax and salt-cured salmon are prepared in much the same way, except the proportions of salt and sugar are reversed. Dill is optional with the salt-cured kind. We've chosen to put the dill in the stewed potatoes instead.

Serves 8 as main, 15 as starter

1 kg salmon fillet, ideally from the thickest part, with its skin
1 dl sugar
0.6 dl coarse salt with iodine, blended or crushed in a mortar

Take away the bones with tongs. Mix sugar and salt and massage into the fish fillet. Put the salmon in a sealed plastic bag and leave on a plate at room temperature for about 2 hours to let the flavour mix melt. Put the plate in the fridge for 24 hours, turning the fish about 3 times. Take it out, dry off and slice thinly.

Stewed potatoes with dill

1 kg boiled potatoes
1 litre milk
6 tbsp cornstarch
2 tbsp water
salt, freshly ground white pepper
1 dl chopped dill

Boil the milk. Dissolve the cornstarch in water, then whisk it into the milk so that the mixture thickens. Season with salt and white pepper. Slice the potatoes, pour the sauce over them and heat briefly. Add the dill just before serving.

Mustard herring

In Danish folklore, mustard makes women reckless. Let's just move on without commenting on our southern neighbours' beliefs! But it can be noted that mustard has long been in use in Sweden, both medicinally (in poultices for snakebites) and gastronomically. And once you've made your own mustard herring, you'll never be tempted by the store-bought kind again. The base is the same 1–2–3 formula as for standard pickled herring: 1 part spirit vinegar, 2 parts sugar, 3 parts water. Mustard sauce also works well as a salmon sauce as an alternative to Head waiter sauce.

Serves 8 as a starter

3–4 fillets of salt herring, soaked in water overnight

Pickling brine

1/2 dl spirit vinegar, 12%
1 dl sugar
1 1/2 dl water

Mustard sauce

1 tsp green peppercorns in brine
2 tbsp Dijon mustard
2 tbsp mild mustard
1 tbsp sugar
1 1/4 dl cooking oil
1 tsp pink peppercorns
1 tsp grated horseradish

Cut the herring fillets into diagonals about the size of dominoes. Put in a glass jar. Warm the vinegar and sugar until the sugar dissolves. Add cold water and make sure that the brine isn't too hot when you pour it over the herring. Cover the fish with the brine and put a saucer or similar weight to press it down. Store in the fridge for 2 days.
Mix the green peppercorns, sugar and mustard. Drizzle in oil while whisking strongly. Mix in the horseradish and pink peppercorns.
Drain the herring in a colander. Mix it with the mustard sauce. Store in the fridge for another 24 hours. Refrigerated, it will keep for about a week.

Fried Baltic herring with potato puree

What is special about Baltic herring? It has the same classification as ordinary herring: *Clupea harengus*. It's the same fish, just that when it is caught north of Kalmar Sound in the Baltic, Swedes call it by another name. Baltic herring is half the size of the standard herring, which can grow to a length of 40 cm/15 in.

Serves 4

500 g fillets of Baltic herring (substitute small herring)
1 dl Dijon mustard
1 dl finely chopped dill

1 dl stoneground rye flour
3 tbsp butter
3 tbsp cooking oil
salt, freshly ground white pepper

Serve with

potato puree
instant pickled cucumber

Snip the back fin off the herring fillets, keeping the back skin intact. On greaseproof paper, spread the fillets flat, skin side down.
Mix the mustard and dill and spread thinly on the fillets. Put them back together with the skin side out. Put 1 tablespoon butter and 1 tablespoon oil into a medium-hot frying pan. Pat the herring with the flour. When the butter stops sizzling, fry the fish 4–5 minutes on each side. Season with salt and white pepper.

Potato puree

500 g peeled potato (preferably a floury variety like King Edward)
2 tsp salt
1 tsp sugar

1 1/2 dl milk
75 g butter
freshly ground white pepper
grated nutmeg (optional)

Boil the potatoes until soft. Pour off the water and let the potatoes steam off. Add salt, white pepper, sugar, nutmeg if you like, butter and milk. Mash with a potato masher until smooth, adding milk to get the consistency you want.

Instant pickled cucumber

1/2 cucumber
1/2 dl finely chopped parsley
1/2 dl spirit vinegar, 12 %

1 dl sugar
1 1/2 dl water

Slice the cucumber as thin as possible. Put it in a jar with the parsley. Boil the vinegar and sugar, then add cold water. Pour over the cucumber. Store in a cool place for at least a couple of hours.

Smoked salmon with creamed spinach and poached egg

Smoked salmon generally means "cold-smoked". Originally, there was only wild salmon but now it's farmed up and down the Swedish coast. Smoke-curing fish was a way of preserving it. In northern Sweden, salt was less available than in the south, so drying and curing were common for stocking the winter larder. Smoked salmon served with poached eggs and spinach is a classic combo.

Serves 4

500 g cold-smoked salmon, thinly sliced

Creamed spinach

500 g fresh spinach
2 dl water
1 tsp salt
1 dl double cream
salt, freshly ground white pepper

Boil the water with the salt. Put in the rinsed spinach leaves. Bring to a boil, then remove the spinach immediately. Let drain in a colander. In a saucepan, bring the cream to a boil, then add the spinach. Season with salt and white pepper.

Poached eggs

4 fresh eggs
2 1/2 tbsp salt
4 tsp spirit vinegar, 12%
2 litres water

Boil water with 4 teaspoons salt and 2 teaspoons spirit vinegar per litre (2 pints) of water. Break each egg carefully into a teacup. Slide the egg into the water, lower the heat, shape the poached eggs with a spoon, and simmer for approx. 4–5 minutes. Remove and drain. Poach the eggs two at a time.

Pickled fried Baltic herring

When frying Baltic herring for dinner, fry a few extra and save for pickling. Pickled fried herring are served cold, traditionally on a Christmas smorgasbord, but are good any time of year. It's also a sheer delight as a simple late-night snack on a piece of crispbread.

Serves 6–8 as a starter or as a buffet component

12 fried fillets of Baltic herring (see recipe)
1/2 carrot
1 onion
7 cm leek
2 bay leaves
1 tsp coarsely ground allspice
1/2 tsp coarsely ground white peppar
1/2 tsp coarsely ground black peppar

Pickling brine

1 dl spirit vinegar, 12%
2 dl sugar
3 dl water

Cut the carrot in half lengthwise. Slice into thin half-moons. Slice the onion and — extra thinly — the leek.
Heat the vinegar and sugar until the sugar dissolves. Add the cold water and let cool. In a bowl, layer the herring and the vegetables and add the spices. Cover with the brine. Put a small plate or saucer on the herring so it is pressed down. Store in the fridge for 2 days.
Refrigerated, it will keep at least a week. Serve with crispbread (see recipe) and boiled potatoes. Beer is a good accompaniment, or even *aquavit*.

Västerbotten pie with vendace roe

This works well as a starter, especially with a dollop of vendace roe (*Coregonus albula*). It will also do well as a buffet dish accompanied by fine smoked ham, salmon or tender asparagus. Västerbotten pie often shows up at crayfish feasts. The name comes from the cheese used for the filling. If you can't find Västerbotten, use another fully matured cheese. You don't have to pre-bake the pie crust. Serves 8.

Pie crust
3 dl white flour
125 g butter
2–3 tbsp water

Filling
1 onion
1 1/2 tsp caraway seeds
3 cl vodka
3 eggs
1 1/2 dl double cream
1 1/2 dl milk
300 g Västerbotten cheese or cheddar, coarsely grated
1/2 tsp salt, freshly ground white pepper
a few drops of Tabasco

Serve with
100 g vendace roe

Drain the roe for a couple of hours, in a coffee filter or on kitchen paper in a colander. You want to be able to shape it into "eggs" for presentation.
Chop the butter into the flour, easiest done in a blender. Add water. Work into a smooth dough. Let rest in the fridge about 30 minutes.
Heat your oven to 200C/400F/GM6. Roll out the dough into a round shape and place in a greased pie dish or a springform pan with removable sides and about 25 cm/10 in in diameter.
Chop the onion and sizzle in a pan with caraway seeds and a little butter until golden brown. Whisk together the eggs, cream, milk, vodka and the coarsely grated cheese. Season with salt, white pepper and Tabasco. Pour the filling into the pie crust. Bake on the lowest rung about 45 minutes or until the filling has set. Serve the pie slightly warm with a dollop of roe.

FOREST AND LAKE

The cousins are gathered in the spacious country kitchen. On the stove, *kropp-kakor* dumplings simmer in a big pan while grandma methodically mixes sugar and lingonberries. Instant preserve, the best way to eat the berries. She baked her cinnamon rolls earlier and while at it, a couple of trays of plain cookies for coffee — that's boiled coffee, if you don't mind. She wipes her hands on her apron and adjusts the grey bun on her neck. Almost time to eat!

It's a special weekend. Not because of the food — grandma is always at the stove preparing something. It's because the cousins have come to help granddad and grandma plant fir trees. After eating, everyone changes into work clothes; suits are discarded for tough denim and high-heeled office pumps for thick boots.

The cleared space in the forest has a warm, heavy scent. Several tall trees have been left; granddad doesn't like clear-cutting and has looked after his forest with inherited skill. It would have been more profitable to use machines that tore down everything at once, but what good is money hoarded at the bank compared to keeping your landscape beautiful?

But replanting at granddad's age required strength that just wasn't there any more. So the grandchildren put up their hands to do it. As a tangible thank-you to their grandparents. To grandma for countless bags of buns and bottles of cordial and cheesecake puddings, baked to perfection in the wood oven. To grandma for never seeing the kids skulking around the outhouse, tummies full of cherries, even though they had been strictly told to "save your appetite for dinner". Or for pretending not to hear kids opening the little burgundy-red porcelain jar in the drawing room to purloin candy: aniseed-y *Kungen av Danmark* or *sidenkuddar* ("silk pillows"). And to thank granddad for the stories about shady horse traders and subjects that grandma thought "the girl" shouldn't hear. That's why the grandchildren were planting fir.

Whether it's a Swede in his own forest or a tourist investigating our fantastic Right of Public Access, we can all enjoy the forest's quiet. Hike with a purpose or just wander about. Kick at some leaves and you might uncover an overlooked line of chanterelle mushrooms. Fill your pockets (bringing an empty bag is the kiss of death — you won't find any), go home and fry them in butter for dinner. Happiness? Yes indeed. Hunkering down in the forest floor on a hot day picking blueberries for a blueberry crumble to follow the fried perch you caught with a hook and a worm in the lake. The lake and the forest are one. Lakes nourish the pine,

Lingonberry shrub in Östergötland.

The pantry

Elk (moose)
Venison
Crayfish
Lingonberries
Blueberries
Perch
Pike
Pike-perch
Burbot
Cucumber
Crispbread
Wild mushrooms

the fir and the oak. Birches mirror their white bark in the waters and drape long branches over the surface.

When the inland ice melted it left about a hundred thousand lakes. The ice was three kilometres thick and pressed down on the land; in 2000 BC, the provinces of Södermanland and Uppland were 20 metres lower than now. The land is still rising, a half centimetre per year in this part of the country. Once again, the only constant is change.

Sea people chuckle contemptuously at lake aficionados: "Still waters? Give us a break!" That's the point, counter the lake people: water for a summer evening dip, for safe skating in winter and to placidly row in a flat-bottomed dinghy on the first day of spring.

And that's not to mention fishing for freshwater crayfish on August nights: setting out crayfish traps under a full moon, with kerosene lanterns and adventure for all ages. Early next morning, you pull up them to see how many little guys have crept into the traps. You count and you measure; small ones get tossed back to grow. The rest are taken home to boil in salty water flavoured with crown dill. As with meatballs, there are countless variations on how to boil. The crescendo comes with the evening's feast, the *kräftskiva*. Dark red crayfish on big dishes, silly paper hats and tables decorated with smirking paper moons. (There's always a snooty someone who won't wear a paper hat.) There's home-flavoured aquavit, *brännvin*, and large Västerbotten cheeses and toast, maybe Västerbotten pie — and raucous, hilarious, occasionally ribald *snaps* songs, short and long, sung solo or in loud, tipsy chorus. For a foreign visitor, it must seem like a twisted kids' party, only with adults.

The *kräftskiva* feast is almost uniquely Swedish. Freshwater crayfish are eaten in other parts of the world — Germany and the American south, for example — but nowhere does the freshwater crayfish have the same cult status. A Swedish tradition began to take shape in the mid-1800s among the upper class. It spread, taking the crayfish feast into the public domain. When the European crayfish (*Astacus astacus*, also known as the noble crayfish) was slowly decimated by crayfish plague, the signal crayfish (*Pacifastacus leniusculus*) was introduced and by the 1970s was the most common species in Swedish lakes. But there aren't enough to go round and at the feasts you'll find mostly American, Turkish or Chinese crayfish, imported deep-frozen. If you want the real thing, try a half-dozen of the Swedish sort. And get busy poking out tiny bits of tasty meat in between *snaps* songs.

Although so much of Sweden is close to the sea, Swedes still think of their home as a land of forests and lakes. Feted author August Strindberg must get some of the blame: he proposed the Swedish flag be changed to green and red instead of

Hamra national park in Dalarna.

The parish of Döderhult in Småland.

yellow and blue — green for the forests and red for the red wooden houses.

Sweden has only two provinces with neither coast nor foreign border: Västmanland and little Närke, which are also next to each other. Närke was home to Cajsa Warg (1703–69), the woman who largely shaped Swedish gastronomy. Christina Warg was born in Närke and was nicknamed Cajsa. She moved to Stockholm as household manager to fine families. In 1755 she published a classic cookbook, *Household Help for Young Women*. Her famous aphorism is, "Use what you've got." (In fact, she really said: "Use what you can get," which is different.) Back in Närke in 1810, the nation's elected representatives met and voted to request Napoleonic marshal Jean Baptiste Bernadotte that he assume the throne of Sweden. His offspring are still here, cutting ribbons, feeding the paparazzi and waving to people.

In that century the landscape started to acquire its current look. Farmers partially drained Lake Hjälmaren to gain an extra 30,000 hectares of arable land. Local diet adapted to what the fields gave: barley, oats, wheat and potatoes. From Hjälmaren and Lake Vättern, whose northern tip pokes into Närke, come pike, pike-perch, eel and perch, salmon and char, of which much is exported. Typical dishes in the region are white cabbage soup, bean soup and *ängamat*, a gorgeous soup with lightly boiled carrots, peas and spinach. Even the doughty *skomakarlåda*, "cobbler's box", comes from Närke where the city of Örebro was once famous for shoe factories. Much of Sweden's supply of sausage and hot dog buns comes from here; the Korvbrödsbagaren factory gets through 48 tonnes of white flour per day. Cordial, fruit fool, sauces, cookies and waffle mix are other top sellers. And 99 per cent of the base essence for Sweden's sweet, dark Christmas pop, *julmust*, is made by the Roberts company in Närke. The region is nicknamed the Whine Belt, *gnällbältet*, but that's for the slightly nasal accent, because the locals certainly cannot complain about the food.

Heading north we come to Västmanland province with its stewed burbot, pike-perch from Lake Mälaren, venison, chanterelles and the mineral springs and bottlers at Loka. Grythyttan is prominent on Sweden's gastronomic map with its cooking college and gourmet inn. If you want an historic local dish, order dumplings with eggs and crispy salted pork.

Much of the province goes under the name of Bergslagen, where over a hundred iron mines were in operation in the 1700s. In its heyday in the 1500s, the silver mine at Sala was the world's richest. Food traditions reflect life in the mining communities. The best preserved is the Engelsberg ironworks, which has been restored and opened to visitors. It is of course on the UNESCO World Heritage List. In the forests, men watched over their smoking charcoal stacks night and day. The foundries swallowed huge amounts of charcoal. The men who watched at night have been immortalised in folksong.

Västmanland's official province animal is the deer, which tells us something about the wealth of game in the forests. A favourite accompaniment for venison is chanterelles, picked wild in the woods. Another classic is pickled cucumber; at one time, cucumber used to be synonymous with the stubby, local Västerås variety. There is still plenty on offer. The city of Västerås is at the northern end of Lake Mälaren and pike-perch from the lake is a real delicacy whether baked in paper or simmered in cream.

Gästrikland province, nudging against Västmanland from the south, does have a Baltic coast, but its interior is all forestry and iron. More than 30 foundries operated here in the 1800s and with Gävle as distribution port, made handsome profits. The mines have long since closed and only a few ironworks survive, with Sandvik AB the biggest.

The elk (moose) on the province's coat of arms indicates bountiful game in the forests; berry and wild mushroom pickers have to be alert during the autumn hunting season. Forestry worker households learned to put everything to use, and a traditional meal was *ärtklubb*, a stodgy dish in which yellow pea flour, barley and milk were whisked together and boiled into a goo. You needed sustenance like that for the long hours working in the forest.

Along the coast, food traditions were obviously influenced by the sea, with seared Baltic herring and mashed potatoes as a favourite combo. Fisherman-farmers used to smoke Baltic herring with juniper to produce shiny *böckling*. Harbour life was centred in Gävle, although now the old fishy smells have since been replaced by others from the Gevalia coffee-roasting complex and the candy factory making the coloured Ahlgrens candy "cars" that Swedes chew on at the movies.

Dalarna province, west of Gästrikland, has a mountain chain towards the Norwegian border and is otherwise dominated by forests and lakes. Dalarna is soaked in culture; this was where Sweden's national romantic movement was nourished, helped by painters Anders Zorn and Carl Larsson. While the former painted nude farmer girls, the latter painted enticing images of fully clothed family togetherness with plentiful children and flowers. Many composers, writers and local historians also contributed, making it easy to understand why Dalarna has a special place in Swedish hearts.

If we had to name one dish from Dalarna it would have to be the lightly smoked and boiled *falukorv* sausage. One story is that the meat originally came from animals no longer able to pull trolleys in the mines. The recipe was said to be a secret one developed by immigrant Germans working at the Stora Kopparbergs Bergslag Company, an enterprise founded in the 1200s. Both the mine and the city of Falun are now on the UNESCO World Heritage List. In a sense, that puts the *falukorv* on the world heritage list too.

The land around Lake Siljan is fertile and beautiful, along the Dalälven River too. Much of the province's best food comes from forest and lake. The hunters' bounty — mostly elk (moose), wood grouse and black grouse — is often cooked with mushrooms, and the lakes provide char and delicate vendace. Dalarna has several well-known crispbread bakeries, among them Vikabröd and the rising star, Pyramid, founded by an immigrant Egyptian who fell in love with a local girl. That's one more way to create regional gastronomy! And crispbread gives us a segue to the province to the southwest, Värmland.

That's because Värmland has the giant Wasabröd bakery in Filipstad where they bake 200 tonnes of crispbread a day. This is the Promised Land of crispbread but also has abundant game in its vast forests. Värmland has almost all species of wild animal that live in Sweden and foodies can enjoy everything from elk and bear to hare and beaver. Or splash out with roast grouse and stewed wild mushrooms for a dinner party. Dalarna has copyright on the *falukorv* sausage but there's a local *Värmlandskorv*, fine and juicy, often served with mashed swedes. Feel like a coffee afterwards, from locally roasted beans? The Löfbergs Lila coffee company will probably be the provider. The company's lilac logo is visible on TV all winter long on the shirts of the successful Färjestad ice-hockey team.

Taking a giant step over the Västgöta Plain we end our forest and lake expedition where we started, in Småland province, with its large forests, low vegetation red with lingonberries, and over 3,000 large and small lakes. For years, this was a province with widespread poverty and in the 1800s large numbers quit failed harvests and misery to seek fortunes across the sea in what they called "The America". Many remained in poverty, and when they threw parties, these people did not hold back. *Kroppkakor* dumplings with lingonberry jam, tangy *isterband* sausage made from barley grain, pork, onion and spices, and newly baked cheesecake pudding with preserves were often on the smorgasbord. And for children living close to Gränna on the shore of Lake Vättern there was the occasional promise of *polkagris* ("polka pig"), white-and-red striped rock candy lollipops.

Swedes call a part of Småland the "kingdom of glass" and glass objects of highest international class have long been produced here. Glassworkers would heat their salted herring and potatoes by the hot ovens. *Hyttsill*, a herring dish named for the practice, currently attracts tourists.

Bags packed with glass purchases from Orrefors, Kosta and other famous glassworks, we return to where those fir trees and pine were planted more than thirty years ago. A catastrophic storm in 2005 felled a huge number of trees but could not ruffle our love for the forest.

Ljurhalla, Västergötland.

Lindström burgers with parsley butter

Lindström's identity is still disputed. There are at least half a dozen stories. Among candidates are Maria Kristina Lindström who ran a café in Stockholm in the mid-1800s, an editor-in-chief, two actors, a schoolteacher from Öster-sund and the Swedish-speaking Finn, Lieutenant Henrik Lindström. In that version, on 4 May 1862, Lieutenant Lindström sat down to dine at the Hotell Witt in Kalmar, southern Sweden. He ordered steak tartare with all the traditional trimmings. He mixed everything together and told the chef to sear it lightly in a frying pan. Whoever Lindström really was, the result is delicious.

Serves 4
1 onion
1–2 pickled beetroots + brine
1–2 cold boiled potatoes
400 g minced beef
3 eggs
1 dl cream
3 tbsp capers
salt, freshly ground white pepper
oil and butter for frying

Serve with
boiled potatoes
parsley butter

Peel and chop the onion. Fry in a little butter. Dice the drained beets and grate the potatoes.
Salt and pepper the mince and blend. Mix in the eggs, cream, potato, beetroot and capers. Smoothen the mix by adding a little beetroot brine. Test-fry a dollop and taste to see if the seasoning is right. Shape 12 patties and fry in butter mixed with a little oil. Serve with parsley butter and boiled potatoes.

Parsley butter
100 g butter, room temperature
1 tsp lemon juice
1 tsp Dijon mustard
2 tbsp finely chopped parsley

Mix all the ingredients for the parsley butter. Form into a snake, wrap in greaseproof paper or clingfilm and put in the fridge.

Beef Rydberg

This luxury version of Sweden's ubiquitous *pyttipanna*, meat-and-potato hash, was created at the venerable old Hôtel Rydberg in Stockholm. The hotel opened its doors in 1857, built on a legacy left by a rich businessman, Abraham Rydberg. The will stated that the money was for an "hôtel de ville", i.e. a city hall. The builder was poor at French, or pretended to be, and interpreted it as "city hotel". The hotel was pulled down in 1914, but Biff Rydberg lives on. Fillet of beef may be over-the-top extravagant, but take the point or "tail" of the fillet and you'll be making use of the whole cut.

Serves 4

500 g fillet of beef
2–3 onions
8 potatoes
4 tbsp butter + 2 tbsp rapeseed oil
salt and freshly ground black pepper

Serve with

parsley
mustard crème
4 raw egg yolks
freshly grated horseradish

Dice the meat into thumbnail-size cubes. Chop the onion. In a frying pan, sizzle the onion in 1 tablespoon butter until golden brown. Peel the potatoes and dice them, slightly smaller than the meat. Fry in 2 tablespoons butter and a little oil. Season generously with salt and black pepper.
Finally, snap-fry the meat on its own at high heat. Arrange everything in separate segments on warmed plates. Garnish with chopped parsley. Serve with raw egg yolks, grated horseradish and mustard crème. Guests create individual mixes.

Mustard crème

1 dl crème fraîche or sour cream
1 tsp Dijon mustard
1 tsp sugar

Mix and serve alongside.

Veal or lamb in dill sauce

Any definition of specific Swedish flavours returns to an interface between sweet and sour. Dillweed arrived in the Nordic region in the early Middle Ages via monastery gardens, and in the early 1600s it was being referred to as "indispensible for pickling". Veal or lamb in dill sauce is a cherished favourite and legendary restaurateur Cajsa Warg (1703–69) created the seminal recipe. Use either veal or lamb and watch grateful Swedes go nostalgic in a flash!

Serves 4

700–800 g shoulder, breast, neck or flank of veal or lamb
100 g celeriac
1/2 leek
2 carrots
1 1/2 tbsp salt
1 bay leaf
7–8 whole white peppercorns

Dice the meat into postage-stamp-size cubes. Cover with water and bring to a boil, skimming off the foam. Pour off the water and rinse under a cold tap. Return the meat to the pot. Cover with water again. Dice the vegetables and add them to the pot with the bay leaf, salt and peppercorns. Bring to a boil, then simmer for about 45 minutes until the meat is tender.

The sauce

5 dl of the cooking liquor
1 dl double cream
juice of 1/2 lemon
1 1/2 tbsp spirit vinegar, 12%
2 tbsp sugar
3 tbsp cornstarch dissolved in a little cold water
1 big bunch of fresh dill
salt and freshly ground white pepper

Strain the cooking liquor and bring to a boil with cream, lemon juice, spirit vinegar and sugar. Season with salt and white pepper. Thicken with the cornstarch mixture. Chop the dill and add. Mix with the meat and serve with boiled potatoes.

Christmas ham

The centrepiece of the Swedish Christmas smorgasbord is the ham. For best results boil the ham yourself. To be über-traditional, save and reduce the cooking liquor for *dopp i grytan*: that's when you dip Swedish rye bread in the pot. Or save the liquor for green kale soup (see recipe), a popular midwinter dish. If you buy your ham ready-boiled, cut away the rind before grilling but leave most of the fat.

Serves 12–15
4 kg salt-cured boneless ham
1 onion
1 carrot
2 bay leaves
10–15 black peppercorns

Mustard crust
4 tbsp strong, sweet mustard
1 tbsp Dijon mustard
2 egg yolks
1 dl breadcrumbs
50 g butter

Put the ham in a large cauldron with sliced carrots and onions, bay leaves and peppercorns. Cover with water. Poke a meat thermometer into the thickest part and simmer until the inside temperature reaches 68C/155F — roughly two hours. Lift out the ham and cut away the rind. Leave to cool overnight. Heat the oven to 300C/575F/GM9. Score a grid pattern in the remaining fat. Mix the mustard and egg yolks and spread onto the ham. Sift over breadcrumbs. Melt the butter and spoon it gently over the breadcrumbs. Grill the ham approx. 10 minutes. Let cool.

Beef stew with allspice

Kalops is a word borrowed from the old English "collops": small pieces or slices of meat. And that word may come from "coal" and "hop" — meat fried so fast it hops from the pan. *Kalops* is usually made from pounded slices of beef, while *kalops* in the Skåne style, like our version, uses diced beef.

Serves 4

1.2 kg chuck or shoulder in stewing chunks
2–3 onions
2 carrots
1–2 tbsp butter
12–15 whole allspice
6 white peppercorns
2–3 bay leaves
1 cube beef stock
3 tbsp cornstarch
salt, freshly ground white pepper

Serve with

pickled beetroot
boiled potatoes

Sear the meat in an iron pot or a large saucepan. Cut the onions into segments and the carrots into short lengths and sear them with the meat. Cover with water. Add the allspice, white pepper and bay leaf. Boil for 90 minutes under a lid.
Dissolve the cornstarch with a little water and thicken the stew with it.
Season with salt and pepper. Serve with boiled potatoes and pickled beetroot.

Pickled beetroot

12–15 small beetroots
salt
1 dl spirit vinegar, 12%
2 dl sugar
3 dl water
3–4 whole allspice
3–4 whole white peppercorns

Boil the beetroots in lightly salted water until soft. Pour off the water and peel the beets. Put in a jar.
Bring to a boil: vinegar, sugar, water, and spices. Stir until the sugar dissolves. Let cool. Pour over the beetroots. Cover and store cold, ideally overnight.

Stuffed potato dumplings and lingonberries

Kroppkakor literally means "body cakes"— an apt name for the pale, round dumplings. Beginners use boiled potatoes, the way they do in Småland province. But the fancier Öland Island style mixes boiled and grated raw potatoes. (Remember to increase cooking time.) Choose a firm potato variety, like the creamy, yellow-fleshed Bintje. Save a little of the fried filling to serve as a side. If there are any *kroppkakor* left, refrigerate. The next day, you cut them in half and fry.

Serves 8	3 litres cold boiled potatoes	2 tsp salt + salt for the cooking liquor
	6 dl white flour	2 tsp sugar
	2 eggs	

For the filling	200 g salt-cured pork belly/smoked ham	freshly ground allspice
	4 tbsp finely chopped onion	freshly ground white pepper

Serve with	instant lingonberry preserve	(also optional: 2 dl cream or
	(optional: surplus filling)	clarified butter)

Boil the potatoes in their jackets. Let them cool — easiest is to boil them the previous day. Peel and mash. If using freshly boiled potatoes, press through a ricer and let cool.

Finely dice the pork or ham. Fry up the filling, spicing generously — the allspice taste must be recognisable. Let the filling cool.

Mix the mashed potatoes, flour and spices on a work surface. Don't use all the flour at once. Make a hole in the middle and break the eggs into it. Quickly work the eggs into the dough, leaving it rather loose — if you work it too long, it'll get sticky. Make a roll, about 7 cm/2 in thick, using all the dough or half at a time. Slice, make a hole in the middle, fill it and pinch shut.

Boil up salted water in two large pots. Drop a dumpling into the water to test the firmness and the water's salinity. Taste check. If the balls are too loose and flaky, roll the rest in a little more flour.

Boil in batches so the dumplings can all float up together. *Kroppkakor* made with only boiled potatoes need to simmer for 10–15 minutes, while the Öland kind involving raw potato will need about 45 minutes. Fish them up with a slotted spoon and drain. Keep them warm under kitchen foil. Add a little salt to the water and do the next batch.

Serve with the filling you saved, cooked up with cream as a sauce. Many Swedes just go with clarified butter.

Mix the lingonberries with as much sugar as tastebuds tell you. Stir until the sugar loses its crunch as it dissolves.

Cabbage dolmas

There are two theories for how one of the 20th-century's most common Swedish dishes is named for the Turkish dolma. The most popular story is that soldiers fighting one of King Karl XII's expeditionary wars were camped near Bender in Turkey long enough to learn to make the dish, then brought it home. (Battling gourmets??) But more credibly, the dish was popularised by the delegations of Turks sent to Sweden between 1716 and '32 to try to get King Karl to repay debts. While in Sweden, they are known to have made many friends. Vary the standard white cabbage with Savoy or Wild cabbage. For easier handling, insert a corkscrew into the thick part of the cabbage before putting it in the water. You can then lift it out and peel off the leaves.

Serves 4

400 g mixed mince (3 parts beef, and 1 part pork)
1 onion
2 dl boiled rice
2 dl double cream
1 egg
5 tbsp butter
1 1/2 tsp salt, freshly ground white pepper
1 big head of white cabbage
dark syrup

Serve with

lingonberry preserve

Put the mince in a big bowl. Peel and chop the onion and add, together with the rice, cream and egg. Season with salt and white pepper.
Cut out and remove the cabbage spine. Boil the whole head in plentiful, slightly salted water 25–30 minutes or until the leaves are soft and transparent. Take out and gently peel off leaves under cold running water. Select 8 large leaves, lay them flat and cut away the thick main vein.
Set your oven to 300C/575F/GM9. Divide the meat onto the leaves, then wrap, folding first, then rolling. Grease an ovenproof dish. Place the dolmas in the dish with the joins down and dot with butter. Bake low in the oven for 35–40 minutes or until the dolmas are darkly coloured. Five minutes before the end, drip a little syrup over them, but watch they don't burn. Serve with lingonberry preserve.

Meatballs with mashed potatoes and lingonberries

The most Swedish dish of them all? The first mention came in the legendary Cajsa Warg cookbook of 1755. By then, home meat grinders had been invented, simplifying kitchen chores and making mince possible. Many nations boast a signature meatball, but this is the way Swedes remember mama's. Mineral water makes the mix nicely porous.

Serves 4

1 1/2 dl milk	1 tsp sugar
1 dl breadcrumbs	1–2 tsp Dijon mustard
1 small onion	2 eggs
500 g mince (3 parts beef, 1 part pork)	2 tbsp butter
1 1/2 tsp salt	1/2 dl carbonated mineral water
1/2 tsp freshly ground white pepper	butter + rapeseed oil for frying

Pour the milk over the breadcrumbs and leave to swell 5–10 minutes. Chop the onion and fry it golden brown in a little butter. Mix into the mince: salt, white pepper, sugar and mustard. Add the egg, milk mixture and onion. Mix until smooth. Splash on some mineral water. Test-fry a teaspoonful and add more seasoning if needed. Roll into large cherry-size and fry in butter and a little oil. Serve with mashed potatoes and instant lingonberry preserve.

Potato mash

500 g peeled potato, ideally a floury sort like King Edward
2 tsp salt
1 tsp sugar
1 1/2 dl milk
75 g butter
freshly ground white pepper
grated nutmeg (optional)

Boil the potatoes until soft. Pour off the water and let the potatoes steam in the saucepan. Add salt, white pepper, sugar, butter, milk and, optionally, nutmeg. Mash with a potato masher. Add more milk if needed to make the mash smooth. Taste and season more if needed.

Instant lingonberry preserve

500 g lingonberries
1 dl sugar

Mix the lingonberries and sugar by hand and stir until the sugar dissolves.

Swedish hash

Another Swedish culinary icon. The Swedish word *pyttipanna* originally meant "push-into-pan" — i.e., toss in what you've got: leftover potatoes, onion and meat, and slow-fry. The classic accompaniment is a raw egg yolk or a fried egg. Serve with pickled beetroot. The dish gets an extra kick with HP sauce.

Serves 4

8 boiled potatoes
approx. 400 g cooked meat, mix of smoked, boiled and salt-cured
2 onions
2 tbsp butter and cooking oil
2 tbsp mild chilli sauce
salt, pepper

Serve with

4 fried eggs
pickled beetroot
HP sauce

Dice the potatoes and meat finely (pinky-nail-size). Chop the onion and sear it in butter and oil. Add the potatoes and meat and fry. Season at the end with salt, pepper and chilli sauce.
Serve with fried eggs and pickled beetroot.

Potato cakes and bacon

The next time you make potato mash, make extra and you'll have the base for Swedish potato cakes. Shredded bacon in the batter mix adds taste. You can go vegetarian by substituting chopped herbs like parsley for the bacon. Lingonberry preserve and pickled cucumbers are traditional, and delicious, accoutrements.

Serves 4

400 g potato mash (see recipe for fried Baltic herring)
2 eggs
1 dl breadcrumbs
optional: 1 tbsp butter
also optional: 1 tbsp oil

Serve with

250 g bacon
instant lingonberry preserve (see recipe for meatballs)

Make a mash that's almost a puree. Mix the mash with the eggs and form patties. Pat with breadcrumbs.
Fry the bacon. Dry on kitchen paper. Use the bacon fat left in the pan to fry the potato cakes, augmenting with butter and oil. Serve with instant lingonberry preserve.

Potato pancakes and salt pork

Raggmunk translates literally as "hackle doughnut". Some say the rough surface of the small pancakes looks like the raised hackles of an angry dog. The dish itself is a refined version of *rårakor*: grated potato pancakes with no other ingredients. For *raggmunk* in a vegetarian version: lose the pork and fry in rapeseed oil.

Serves 4

300 g salt-cured pork
8 potatoes
2 dl white flour
5 dl milk
1 tsp salt
1/2 tsp white pepper

Serve with

instant lingonberry preserve (see recipe for meatballs)

Fry the pork and drain on kitchen paper, saving the frying fat in the pan. Peel the potatoes and grate fairly fine. Put in a strainer and drain. Whisk together milk and flour and fold in the potatoes. Season with salt and pepper and and fry the *raggmunk* as you would small, thin pancakes. Serve with instant lingonberry preserve.

Salt-cured brisket and mashed swedes

In the old days, Swedes salted meat and fish so they would keep over the winter. An alternative was to salt-cure, which meant a shorter eat-by date. These days we buy brisket ready salt-cured and just boil it up. It still takes time but the result is worth it.

Serves 4

700–800 g salted brisket
2 carrots
100 g celeriac
1 small leek
black peppercorns
1 bay leaf

Cut carrots, celeriac and leek into thick pieces. Put into a pot with the brisket still in one piece. Cover with water. Boil under a lid for 60–90 minutes until the brisket feels tender.
Remove from the pot, cover with a cloth and let cool under a weight — a heavy saucepan on an oven tray, for example. Sieve the cooking liquor and save for the mash.
Slice the brisket and sear quickly in a frying pan. Serve with the swede mash and sprinkle with chopped parsley for presentation.

Swede mash

1 small swede (rutabaga)
2 medium carrots
50 g celeriac
4 potatoes
50 g butter
salt, freshly ground white pepper

Peel and cube the roots and boil in the cooking liquor from the brisket until soft. Mash with a potato masher. Season with butter, salt and pepper, using cooking liquor to thin to a desired consistency.

Cobbler's box

There are several dishes named for trades. In the past, with little opportunity to heat their food properly, tradesmen mixed everything in one metal box and placed it on or close to the fire in the workshop. The meat in a Cobbler's box was said to resemble shoe soles (in looks only, hopefully).

Serves 4

8–10 potatoes
3–4 onions
600 g salted pork belly
2 dl meat broth
butter for frying

Heat the oven to 225C/450F/GM8. Peel and slice the onions and potatoes. Fry separately the onions, potatoes and salted pork belly (or bacon). Layer everything in an oven dish, with potatoes bottom and top. Pour broth over and bake for 30–35 minutes or whenever the potato feels soft.

Knob of venison with blackcurrant jelly

This recipe apparently originated when a woman forgot to thaw her frozen venison. She put it in the oven at low heat (this is before the days of the microwave) but forgot about it until the next morning. In shock, she put the meat into a brine and hoped for the best. The result was magnificent. Beef can also be used. Select a whole piece of shoulder, thick flank, or rumpsteak.

Serves 6-8

1 kg deep-frozen, boneless venison

Brine

1 litre water
1 dl salt
2 tbsp sugar
1 bay leaf
1 tsp crushed black pepper
2 tbsp crushed juniper berries

Place the frozen meat on a grate over a roasting pan. Put everything into a cold oven on the lowest rung. Set the temperature to 100C/220F/GM1/4 and roast for 9–10 hours. Stick a thermometer into the meat after 2 hours and wait for the reading to hit 60C/140F. Take out the meat and put it into a narrow bowl or a thick plastic bag.
Mix the brine ingredients in a saucepan. Bring to a boil. Pour the hot brine over the meat, then cover (or tie up the plastic bag). Store cool for 4–5 hours. Take out the meat, dry and slice it thinly. Serve cold with blackcurrant jelly and boiled potatoes. Or include it in a buffet spread with salad and bread.

Blackcurrant jelly

1 1/2 dl water
1 litre blackcurrants
caster sugar, 9 dl sugar per litre of juice

Boil up the berries and water 5–10 minutes until the berries have released their juice. Sieve and measure the collected juice.
Use 9 dl sugar per litre of juice. Boil until the sugar has dissolved. Pour the jelly into clean, hot jars. Screw on the lids.

Wallenberg burger

These are magically light burgers, all the better for being made with finely minced veal. The recipe was first published by Charles Emil Hagdahl in an ambitious 1879 cookbook. Hagdahl's daughter Amalia married into the powerful Wallenberg finance clan. Amalia loved cooking as much as her father, and this concoction of minced meat, made luxurious by the addition of egg yolks and cream, was named after her.

Serves 4

350 g veal mince
1 1/2 tsp salt
a pinch of freshly ground white pepper
2 dl double cream
4 egg yolks
3 slices of white bread, minus crust
2 tbsp butter

Serve with

potato puree
chanterelle mushrooms fried in butter
green peas
instant lingonberry preserve

Mix the mince with salt and pepper. Add cream and egg yolks. The mix should be slightly loose. Test-fry a dollop and taste.
Pulverise the bread in a blender and put the crumbs on a plate. Shape the burgers on the breadcrumbs and slowly fry in butter until golden brown. Serve with chanterelle mushrooms fried in butter. The classic accopaniments are small green peas, potato puree and lingonberry preserve.

HIGHLAND AND WILDERNESS

For over two hours, he sits silent. He gazes at the horizon and concentrates on the dog sled he's in charge of. Lightly twitching his thumbs, he gets the entire team of Siberian huskies to obey his every command. The sled glides swiftly and weightlessly over frozen snow covered with a thin new layer of powder snow.

The hood of his anorak is drawn close around his face so only a pair of alert, peppercorn-brown eyes peek out. The furry edge of the coat must be tickling his skin, and he occasionally takes the reins in one hand so he can scratch his cheek with the other. But his eyes never leave the dog team.

He is young, probably no older than eighteen, and his face is already weather-beaten. The mountains are his home. He was born here with the wilderness as his backyard. In the background rises Mount Kebnekaise, majestic and secure in its supremacy — at 2,111 metres over sea level it is Sweden's highest mountain. The journey continues without a word. Then, after an eternity for a city person, he turns sideways, nods and says: "Yep."

"What?" his passenger replies. "Yep what?"

"I was answering you," he says, tugging gently at the reins to alter direction slightly. His smile is warm. It's an answer he has obviously given consideration. The problem is that the questioner, used to a higher, urban conversational pace, has long since forgotten the query. The young sled driver sees the perplexed look and recaps:

"You asked if I wanted to stay here. For the rest of my life. Yep, I do. But I'd really like to live even further north. If I could."

After that, not a word until lunch. When the time comes, he stops the sled at a little rest area and starts digging through our kit. Out comes a freshly smoked Arctic char, sliced boiled potato, sour cream, onion and flatbread. He lays the food out so we're facing south to take advantage of the weak sun, and spreads out a couple of large reindeer skin rugs on the snow. Beer and a little hip flask complete the meal.

"Like it?" He nods at the hip flask. "It's my Dad's own mix...he makes it."

The "moonshine" is smooth and tasty and no mention is made of dad's law-breaking ways. The spirits warm us to our toes. And the wrap of flatbread and smoked char has a flavour a world away from the kind you can buy at kiosks in the northern towns.

The wind ploughs furrows through the dogs' long grey fur as they lie stretched out, gathering strength before the next leg. The landscape is almost completely

The pantry

Reindeer
Bear
Elk (moose)
Grouse
Salmon trout
Grayling
Arctic char
(sabling)
Whey cheese
Flatbread
Almond potatoes
Cloudberries
Cranberries

Kebnekaise, the highest mountain in Sweden

white; only the pale blue sky provides contrast. It is so beautiful you could cry.

Of course he's right, our youth of the wilds. Why would anyone want to live further south?

Stockholmers joke that Northern Sweden and its wilderness begin at the old Stallmästargården inn at the highway access barely a kilometre north of the capital's centre. Those jokesters have probably never seen even a postcard of mountains, let alone trekked the wilds. More map-wise people locate the cut-off at the Dalälv River. North of that watercourse the forest expands breathtakingly although still some distance from the real wilderness.

We make our way instead to Härjedalen province, close to the Norwegian border. The province is at an altitude of between 300 and 600 metres with a population density of scarcely one citizen per square kilometre. The altitude means that grain will not grow, orchard harvests are meagre and potatoes need a southern vista to grow. Survival used to depend on getting feed and grazing for cattle. An outpost farming system developed, with farmers driving cattle to the rich pastures of the highland foothills in summer and staying with them. Up there, whoever was watching the cows could make cheese for the winter and churn butter and soft whey cheese. Many of the old huts and pastures have either been preserved for sightseers or turned into cabin resorts for skiing and hiking.

Hunting is part of people's lives here and culinary traditions reflect this. Larded hare and elk (moose) stew are local favourites. Then there's the fish: common whitefish, Arctic char and salmon trout are most common. It's a popular place for anglers, with thousands of lakes, rivers and waterways. The province fish is the grayling but you'll find lots of pike and perch too. And since forever, berries and wild mushrooms have had a dietary role. Härjedalen also has Sweden's southernmost Sami village with reindeer-herding, the traditional Sami livelihood.

We move on north, to the "Republic" of Jämtland — the locals' proud and affectionate name for a province that was long independent of both Sweden and neighbouring Norway. "Independence Day" is celebrated at the Great Lakes Festival (*Storsjöyran*) in Östersund. The forests are grandiose and the mountains rise proudly. Add on the lakes and the mighty rivers that supply Sweden with a major source of hydropower. If you had to choose two prime ingredients from Jämtland, they would be elk (moose) meat and milk. The September elk hunt is almost a sacrament and they say every third local gets involved. Just try to make appointments then! There's also reindeer meat that is smoked, dried and salt-cured or is butchered, hung and deep-frozen, pan-ready.

This province had outpost farming too, with the resultant whey cheeses, hard and soft. Take the local soft flatbread, spread with butter, add slices of the harder whey cheese, then roll it up, and you've made an original *stut*. These days they fancy them up with reindeer meat or smoked salmon. Up in the outposts, they used to make "long-milk", a kind of soured milk with butterwort triggering the acidification process. Most cow and goat cheese used to be made in the outposts but today farmstead dairies produce the wonderful local cheeses, mainly from goat milk.

The barley grown around Storsjön Lake used to go to barley porridge and various kinds of bread; the local softbread is mainly made from barley flour. Similar bread types made further to the south were baked only a couple of times a year and baked to last, but the local bread is a perishable commodity. A few years ago, a baker in Östersund used to give his softbread a "reverse guarantee": "If you've kept it for five days and it hasn't gone mouldy, we'll replace it!" Best enjoyed fresh, in other words.

The lakes and brooks are well filled with highland fish: grayling, char and salmon trout. The wildest waters are close to Tännforsen, Sweden's mightiest waterfall, outside the ski resort of Åre.

On our way up to Lapland we detour deep into Ångermanland. It's a province that sweeps from mountain to coastline. (More in the chapter on Coast and Sea.) We keep to the highlands, close to the forest and its berries, wood mushrooms and game. Feasts would always feature elk (moose) meat or roast black grouse and cloudberries for dessert. In the outposts, the cattle watchers used to eat *kams*, a kind of stuffed dumpling made with milk, soft whey cheese and barley grain. The filling was often pork. These days, grated raw potato is mixed with the barley.

We've made it to Lapland, the province most symbolic of mountains and wilderness. It has been called Europe's last wilderness and is valued enough to make the list of World Heritages as Laponia, which encompasses principally four great national parks — Padjelanta, Sarek, Stora Sjöfallet and Muddus — and the Sjaunja wetlands. From the centre of Laponia, Lake Rissajaure, it's forty-five kilometres to the nearest road. This is a place to feel humble or bask in solitude.

Lapland has no coast but many waterways, together with the vast expanses creating a world where the sea somehow feels unnecessary. There are few towns to disturb the night sky and smaller townships have names that cascade like poetry: Kvikkjåkk, Jokkmokk, Voullerim, Kallatjåkko and Karesuando.

In the town of Ammarnäs you can wrap your mouth around a place name, literally: in the centre of town there's a Potato Hill where the local people grow marvellous potatoes. The Northern Swedish potato that beats them all is the almond potato: long, amber and with a divine flavour. It goes perfectly with *renskav* (thin slices of reindeer meat) stewed in cream or with *souvas*, lightly smoked reindeer brisket.

Left: Kukkolaforsen, Torne älv. Above: Kebnekaise from a helicopter.

The indigenous people, the Sami, know how to make use of every scrap of the animal from the meat to the skin and bones. A classic dish is *lappkok*, a stew of flank, tongue, marrowbone and liver. It is served with reindeer meat sausage, *palt* (bread baked with blood and rye flour) and goat cheese or hard whey cheese.

Here too hunting and fishing are integral and an age-old local favourite is roast bear meat. But gourmets are more attracted to snow grouse and the Arctic char from crystalline mountain lakes.

This far north, the growth season is short. Spring comes late but thanks to the magic summer weeks when the midnight sun keeps darkness at bay, some plant life finds the strength to grow. This is when you can come across Northern Sweden's "gold" — huge wetlands covered in golden brown cloudberries. It's as though a mythical Norse giant had thrown out a huge handful of gold dust, glistening in the dusk. You can also find Arctic raspberries, those exquisite tasting, vitamin C-rich little berries that make delicious preserve or ice cream.

Iron ore brought prosperity — and the wider world — to Lapland, and the city of Kiruna boasts the world's largest underground mine. Some disused mine tunnels conceal a gastronomic oddity: farmed shiitake mushrooms!

Outside Kiruna is Jukkasjärvi, on the global tourist map thanks to the wondrous ice hotel, rebuilt every year to attract hundreds of visitors, especially from Japan.

Directly west of Kiruna there's the rest area where our dogs are impatiently waiting to be hitched up again to the sleds. Lunch break is over and it's time for a last haul to the mountain station right at the foothills of Mount Kebnekaise. The station was built in 1907 but rebuilt in 1991 to include a hotel and restaurant. If you come in summer, you can drive to Nikkaluokta and hike the last 19 kilometres. The more adventurous might like to hike the magnificent 440-kilometre-long Kungsleden Trail.

The dogs are ready. We've packed what is left of our lunch, screwed back the twist-top on the hip flask and spread the reindeer skin rugs in the sleds. Our young sled driver smiles, letting us know with his usual loquacity that it's time to go:

"Well?"

We nod in reply. We're learning.

Kallbygden in Jämtland.

Kale soup

If you're in the right climate zone, kale is easy to grow and can conveniently be left in the ground over the winter. This soup is a real energy booster.
If you don't have your own soup stock handy, boil 3 soup cubes in 1 1/2 litres/3 pints water with a little smoked ham or pork for added taste. For a vegetarian soup, use vegetable soup cubes and omit the smoked pork.

Serves 6

1 bunch fresh kale or 500–700 g deep-frozen
1 1/2 litre soup stock
1 onion, chopped
1/2 tsp fennel seeds
1–2 dl double cream
salt, freshly ground white pepper
5 tbsp cornstarch + 1 dl water

Serve with

hard-boiled eggs, halved

Chop the kale and blanch in boiling, slightly salted water for 1 minute. Drain in a colander.
Boil your stock with the onion and fennel seeds. Add the cream. Dissolve the cornstarch in water and thicken the soup. Add the kale and boil for a minute. Puree in a blender. Season with salt and white pepper. Serve the soup with hard-boiled egg halves.

Yellow pea soup

Pea soup and pork on Thursdays is a tradition dating back to the Middle Ages. Catholic custom made it sinful to eat meat on Fridays so it was wise to eat your fill the day before. Sweden gets most of its yellow peas from Öland Island where pea fields are a conspicuous part of the landscape. The meat used can vary; use what you've got. You can also lose the meat and make it vegetarian, just add a couple of cubes of vegetable stock to the water. Warm punsch liqueur is a traditional accompaniment, and a treat if you're inclined. To be authentically Swedish, end with a dessert of pancakes with preserves (see recipe).

Serves 6

4 dl dried yellow peas
2 litres water
1 big onion
600 g salt-cured, boneless knuckle of pork
2 bay leaves
1 tsp dried marjoram
1 tsp dried thyme
salt and freshly ground white pepper

Serve with

mustard
crispbread
mature cheese

Soak the peas overnight in a cool place. Boil the peas in their soaking water, skimming off the froth and skins when they float to the surface. Chop the onion into segments and add together with the whole knuckle of pork, the bay leaves, the marjoram and the thyme. Boil for 90 minutes.
Take out the meat, dice and put back into the soup. Add more water if the soup is too thick. Serve with mustard, crispbread and cheese.

Punsch

1 litre caster sugar
6 dl water
1 litre vodka
1 bottle of arrack, 37 cl
3/4 tbsp fresh lemon juice

Boil the sugar and water. Let cool. Mix all ingredients. Pour the punsch into clean bottles. Store for about 2 weeks before using. Serve either cold with the after-dinner coffee or warm with pea soup.

Crispbread

Traditionally, Swedes in the far north ate soft, tortilla-type wheat bread. In the far south, a syrup-based bread often of rye was preferred — in the region between, crispbread ruled. In large parts of the country, baking was not done daily, so bread that would keep, like crispbread, was common. And baking it is easier than you might think. Use any flour you want; if you want to go rustic, use stoneground, and if you want to go healthy, use fine rye flour or barley. If the bread loses its crispness, warm it in the oven.

Makes about 20 pieces

25 g fresh yeast (approx. 12 g dried)
4 dl tepid water (37C/99F)
2 tsp salt
2 tsp ground caraway seeds
4 tbsp sesame seeds
4 tbsp sunflower seeds
4 tbsp linseed
7 dl stoneground rye flour
6 dl white flour

When rolling flat

a pinch of gourmet salt
black sesame seeds

Dissolve the yeast in lukewarm water. Add salt, the seeds, and as much flour as you need to make a dough. Put the dough on a work surface and knead for 5–10 minutes. Put in a bowl, cover with plastic film and let rise 30–40 minutes. Take up the dough, divide into four parts and roll out into lengths. Divide each length into five, shape into balls, then roll out into thin, round shapes. Roll in some gourmet salt and black sesame seeds towards the end. (Swedes like to use a patterned rolling pin.) Cover with a cloth and let rise 20 minutes. Heat the oven to 225C/450F/GM8. Bake for about 8 minutes, until the bread is dry and hard. Let cool on a grate. Keep in a sealed container.

Sweetened rye bread

Originally from Skåne and western Sweden. In the 1700s the Swedish navy had similar bread on board as part of provisions, leading to its popularity near port towns. It could last three years but was so hard it had to be moistened with beer or other liquid so the sailors could chew it. The modern, more easily masticated type uses scalded flour. A weight over the bread during baking gives it density. Scalding the flour gives it moistness. Kavring tastes best when it has had a day to settle. Can be deep-frozen.

Makes 3 loaves

Day 1:
5 dl water
3 dl hot coffee
1/2 tbsp ground caraway seeds
1/2 tbsp ground aniseed
1/2 tbsp ground fennel seeds
8 dl stoneground rye flour

Day 2:
50 g butter
4 dl water
50 g fresh yeast (approx. 25 g dried)
1 1/2 tbsp salt
1 tbsp spirit vinegar, 12%
1 dl dark syrup
1.2–1.3 litre stoneground rye flour
ca 1 litre white flour

Day 1: Boil the water and spices. Put the flour in a big bowl and pour in the hot water and coffee, then mix well. Cover with plastic film and leave at room temperature overnight or 10–12 hours.

Day 2: Melt the butter and add to the water and heat to 50C/125F. Pour over the mix from the day before. Crumble in the yeast. Add salt, spirit vinegar and syrup and mix to a loose dough. Work in the rye flour. Then knead in the white flour. Save about 2 dl for working and dusting later. Let rise under a cloth until doubled in size — 2 hours should do it.

Put the dough on a work surface and work in the rest of the flour. Divide the dough into three and shape into even lengths. Put into greased, standard-size loaf tins, punch down and let rise, covered, about 25–30 minutes.

Heat the oven to 225C/450F/GM8. Put the loaf tins low in the oven and cover with greased baking trays, grease side down. Weigh it all down with a heavy frying pan or a brick. Lower the heat to 175C/350F/GM4 and bake for about 55 minutes. Take out the tins and tip the loaves onto a baking tray. Bake another 15–20 minutes. Wrap the bread in clean kitchen cloths and let cool. Store in plastic bags.

Sandwich layer cake

For partygoers in Sweden in the 1970s, sandwich layer cake was part of the experience. Now it's back again. The filling consists of salmon and *böckling* (smoked Baltic herring). You can build your sandwich cake a day in advance, leaving the garnishing until just before presentation. Serves 8–10.

Bread layers

50 g fresh yeast (approx. 25 g dried)
5 dl water, 37C/99F
2 tsp salt, 1 tsp dark syrup
2 tsp cooking oil
3 dl wholewheat flour
10–12 dl white flour

400 g *gravlax* or cold-smoked salmon
1 kg shrimps in their shells
1 egg, hard-boiled
10 cm cucumber, a couple of radishes
romaine or cos lettuce, parsley
butter, a little mineral water

Dissolve the yeast in water. Add salt, syrup, oil and wholewheat flour. Mix in white flour. Knead and put back in a bowl, cover and let rise 45 minutes. Take up the dough, knead and make a round cake. Let it rise in a greased, round dish, ideally a springform pan. Cover and leave for 45 minutes. Heat the oven to 200C/400F/GM6. Bake the bread for about 35 minutes. Cool under a cloth.

Böckling mousse

400 g smoked Baltic herring,
deboned (substitute: kippers)

1 dl mayonnaise
1 dl heavy cream

Cream cheese mix

300 g Philadelphia cream cheese
3 dl crème fraîche or sour cream

1 tsp salt
1/2 tsp freshly ground white pepper

Mustard sauce

1 1/2 tbsp caster sugar
1 1/2 tbsp Dijon mustard

1 1/2 tbsp mild mustard
1 dl cooking oil, a pinch of salt

In a blender, mix herring, mayonnaise and cream until smooth. Mix the cream cheese and crème fraîche. Season with salt and white pepper. Make sure that the ingredients for the sauce are at room temperature, otherwise it will split. Mix sugar and mustard and drizzle in oil. Season with salt. Store in the fridge. Cut the crusts off the loaf and slice into three layers. Put the first on a dish. Moisten with a little mineral water. Spread with mousse and cover with sliced cucumber. Press the next layer down. Next layer: Moisten with mineral water. Spread a little butter, then cover with the salmon, saving a few slices for the garnish. Drizzle over the mustard sauce. Shred a little lettuce. Press the top layer down. Third layer: Moisten with mineral water. Spread the cheese mixture all over the cake. Garnish with salmon, peeled shrimp, egg and sliced radish. Pat shredded lettuce and chopped parsley onto the sides. Sandwich cake benefits from a couple of hours in the fridge before serving.

Elderflower cordial

Cool, pale yellow elderflower cordial is integral to early summer. And it's remarkably easy to make your own. Pick the flowers just before they bloom. An old superstition says this should be done in early morning before the dew has evaporated.

Makes one batch

about 40 flower clusters
2 lemons
2 kg caster sugar
80 g tartaric or citric acid
2 litre boiling water

Rinse the flower clusters carefully to get rid of tiny insects. Put the flowers in a large pan (5–6 litres).
Scrub the lemons and slice thin. Mix lemons, sugar and the tartaric or citric acid in the pan. Pour boiling water over and stir well.
Remove from heat and place the pan in a cool place — a cellar rather than a fridge — with a clean kitchen cloth knotted over as cover. Let stand for 5 days.
Stir every day, pressing the lemon slices against the sides to extract juice.
Strain through cheesecloth or similar. Don't force, allow the syrup to drip.
Collect the pale yellow syrup and refrigerate. The cordial will keep for months.
Pour into plastic bottles if deep-freezing, but fill only halfway because the liquid expands.
Dilute with cool water and serve with lemon or lime slices. Use as a cocktail component or just as a refreshing mealtime drink.

Yuletide mulled wine

Sweden's Christmas *glögg* has been a fixture since the early 1800s and another kind of mulled wine was in use in the 1600s. Alcoholic spirits were poured over a chunk of loaf sugar on a grate, the sugar was lit with a match and melted into a pot below. Then wine and spices were added. The quality of imported wine at the time was iffy and the spices masked the taste. Today, *glögg* is almost exclusively a Christmastime thing and the spices are now there to heighten taste. Traditional accompaniments are ginger biscuits (*pepparkakor*) and, for dunking in the *glögg*, raisins and blanched almonds.

Serves 8

10 cl vodka
4–5 bits of cinnamon stick
20 cloves
a bit of fresh ginger
1 tsp cardamom
1/2 Seville orange peel
1 bottle red wine
1 1/2 dl caster sugar
1 tsp vanilla sugar

Serve with

raisins
almonds, blanched and peeled
ginger biscuits (see recipe)

In a mortar, crush the cinnamon, cloves, ginger, cardamom and Seville orange peel. Transfer to a bowl or jar and pour the vodka over. Cover and let stand for 12–24 hours.
Strain through kitchen paper or a coffee filter.
Mix with wine, sugar and vanilla sugar. Heat (do not boil!) and serve with raisins and blanched almonds.

Snaps

As with *glögg*, spices were once used to hide the taste of fusel oil in poor grain or potato vodka. Today, herbs and spices can provoke delightful flavours. This version of *snaps* works well as an accompaniment to pickled herring or crayfish. Invent concoctions. And instead of shoving herbs into the neck of a bottle — and fighting to retrieve them later — mix everything in a wide-necked jar.

Makes 1 bottle

70 cl plain vodka
1 tsp aniseeds
1 tsp fennel seeds
peel of 1 washed lemon
1 cube of sugar
2 sprigs of fresh mint

Mix everything in a wide jar. Let stand 2–3 days. Strain, then pour into a clean bottle. If you find the taste too pungent, dilute with more plain vodka. Chill and serve.

FIELD AND MEADOW

A child's light feet fly across the field of clover. The scent of summer is rich and sun-soaked. The air is filled with verdure and the girl's sun-tanned legs are marked with band-aids and grazes the way summer legs are.

Swinging from her hand, a plaited basket contains a thermos of coffee, a bottle of elderberry cordial and fresh baked cinnamon rolls. The basket's destination is a field where the first new potatoes are being dug up.

The coffee break is welcome. The potato pickers leave the furrows and make their way to a shaded rock pile by the side of the field. Faces streaked with sweat are wiped, mucky hands are given a perfunctory swipe on blue work pants while eyes turn to the basket. But first they stamp hard on the ground to awaken any drowsy adders lurking among the rocks and get them to move off. But nothing moves; no snakes today.

With a motherly touch, the girl with the basket spreads out the provisions on a chequered kitchen cloth. The coffee and warm rolls are audibly attacked. The girl downs a glass of elderberry cordial, brushes away a sun-bleached tress of hair from her forehead and strides off towards the potato field with the empty basket in her hand. This is what she has been waiting for!

Yes! They remembered! They had left some of the tiniest potatoes for her. She is drawn like a gold-rush miner to the first furrow. She digs with bare fingers into the warm, dark earth, quickly filling her basket with new potatoes the size of cherries.

Proudly, she marches back to the stone pile with a broad, slightly toothless smile, to show off her harvest. Her own potatoes. She races home across the field to scrub them clean with a kitchen brush and boil them in little water and lots of freshly picked dill from the kitchen garden. Then she will eat them hot with a dollop of butter and a little salt. Nothing more. Her own potatoes.

Summer in southern Sweden at the end of the 1960s. It will never be better.

"See in the fields around the lake, the beauty myriad flowers make" wrote Sweden's rambunctious poet Carl Michael Bellman to his love Ulla on a summer day in 1773. The carefree bard possibly gave little thought to the labour invested in every field or meadow. In contrast to the other landscapes described in this book (coast, forest and lake, and highlands and wilderness), field and meadows are tangibly formed by human hand, which together with grazing domestic animals has shaped the country's agricultural scenery. Just how hard we've had to bend our backs to produce workable soil or a lush meadow depends on which part of the country we inhabit.

Haväng, Skåne.

The pantry

Wheat
Barley
Rye
Oats
Potatoes
Elder
Apples
Milk
Pork
Beef
Beans
Onions
Strawberries
Sugar beet
Rapeseed

But the meadows and fields look different today than in Carl Michael Bellman's time. Partly because our tools are so much better, as is the quality of the crops, and partly because the old conical haystacks are long since gone. Hay is no longer dried in situ but packed in huge plastic balls, often white. These lie around the field waiting to be transported to the barn. There's little national romanticism about it but it's more practical for the farmers and allows them to feed cattle "vacuum-packed grass" in the middle of winter. When National Geographic magazine commissioned a photographer to travel around Sweden a few years ago, he found that these gigantic marshmallows typified the country landscape more than anything else.

The greatest change in the farmed landscape in the (roughly) modern era was in the 1800s with the partitioning reform. The idea was praiseworthy: farmers had plots spread out over wide areas and partitioning the land meant that these plots could be consolidated. This was by no means unique to Sweden. But what happened next came to change the landscape forever — and, some claim, Swedish society. It was not enough to redistribute farmland; dwellings were often moved from villages to the new, now cohesive, land holdings. Only a few regions escaped this disaster. However, there are still row villages on Öland Island and in Småland province the village of Stensjö retains its original unity. But for many people, distance to their neighbours increased. When people met, it was as strangers or visitors. Grand farm feasts once or twice a year replaced mundane daily meetings. The feasts were substantial occasions; if meetings were rare, they were to be celebrated. No penny-pinching.

The province Swedes associate more than others with rich harvests is Skåne, Sweden's breadbasket. In 1795, artist and Renaissance man Carl August Ehrensvärd observed that "the native of Skåne has reddish colouring, is well-dressed and at table." And he dined "on good food, much food and punctually." In Skåne, food and culture are integrated. There are few communities without their inn and old culinary traditions are faithfully observed, such as the *Ålagille* eel feast in October and the goose banquets of *Mårten Gås* in November. The *spettekaka* or pyramid cake, that classic Skåne delicacy made from a batter of egg yolk, sugar and flour piped into a lacy cone that is baked until brittle-sticky, was originally a traditional wedding cake. It has been revived and is often served at both small and large parties.

Skåne's fields — we're not talking about tiny plots — supply Sweden with sugar beet, vegetables, fruit, fresh herbs and wheat and other grains. Some of the wheat stays in the province in the town of Åhus to be transformed into Absolut Vodka, Sweden's export mega-hit. In the province's fabled Österlen region, with Kivik as its main town, apples are ubiquitous and on the other side of the province, on the west coast, the Bjäre peninsula produces excellent new potatoes.

If Skåne is the country's bread-basket, the province of Blekinge is its garden. Its leafy woods seem feather-light and airy compared to the dense conifer forests further north. The oak and beech forests are especially pleasant. The farmed landscape is dominated by strawberry and vegetable growing, including huge greenhouses for tomatoes and cucumbers. The city of Karlshamn is known for its margarine and ice-cream but also for the delicately sugary Carlshamn *punsch*. It was first distilled here in the 1700s and is the drink of choice to go with yellow pea soup.

Don't be astonished if you come across ostriches in Blekinge — the plumed giants are raised here alongside pigs, sheep and cattle. Proximity to the sea is reflected in the local gastronomy. Cod is prized here, and often served salt-cured with mustard sauce. But these days, with cods stocks in sharp decline, eating cod has become a moral issue: should you eat other fish in protest until the floating fishing factories learn to take care of our legacy? One alternative is to fish for salmon in the Mörrum River, one of Europe's most famous salmon-angling waters, drawing enthusiasts from far and wide to try their luck. They are seldom disappointed.

Out at sea swim herrings, those that make their way north towards Öland Island accepting a name-change to Baltic herring as they pass Kalmar Sound. At first glance, Öland has a barren look, so its inclusion in a chapter on fields and meadows might seem odd. But in fact the Mörbylånga Valley in the southern part of the island is, alongside Skåne province, the most fertile farming land in the country. Before the postglacial elevation of the land, the entire valley lay under water. What used to be seabed now grows sugar beet, onions, beans, potatoes, strawberries and yellow peas.

North of a fault scarp the expanse known as Stora alvaret stretches out, a 10-by-50-kilometre-large limestone plateau listed as a World Heritage site. To the untrained eye the area appears flat and bland. But take time to enjoy its barren beauty and you'll discover a wealth of rare plants, especially herbs that can be dried for warming winter teas. For residents who remain for the winter, tea in a large, hot mug is a comfort against *Fåken*, Öland's winter wind that piles snow in metre-high drifts.

In years gone by, the wind used to be caught by windmills to mill flour. Today the windmills are left as symbols of a bygone era. The flour and grated raw potato were squeezed into Öland's famous *kroppkakor* dumplings, boiled with a savoury filling. In Småland province the principal ingredient is boiled potato but here it's the raw kind. The *kroppkakor* are small and grey and used to be filled with fish or pork or whatever was at hand.

Grazing sheep are a common sight and Öland lamb rightly has a reputation as a delicacy. Equally good is beef from the cows that chew their fill from the coastal meadows where the feed consists of tasty herbs like wild thyme and Ramsoms (bear garlic). The island has been called the Provence of the North for its variety of flavours and the magical light that has attracted artists over the years.

It has not always been this bucolic. From the 1500s until 1801, Öland was a royal hunting preserve with limited rights for the local population to hunt and farm. There are accounts of actual hunger riots on the island's east in the 1700s and semi-clothed children wandering through villages in winter, begging for food. It is hard to visualise that today, cycling down the village street to buy strawberries for breakfast and picking up a flyer for the autumn's grand occasion, the Öland Harvest Festival. When September turns into October, almost every country barn displays produce for sale to passers-by.

Gotland Island also has rich arable land. The limestone base limits harvests somewhat but the taste of the produce is full compensation. Enjoy a soup made with sand leek (*Allium scorodoprasum*) or wander through a herb garden inhaling the scents. Like Öland, Gotland has grazing sheep (far less common on the mainland) and the two islands both claim to produce the best lamb in Sweden. Gotland's sheep face the weather outdoors year-round, producing fine fleece and good meat. Lamb dishes are numerous and if you're served *glödhoppa* (literally, ember-hop), you're eating seared slices of dried salted leg of mutton that, perhaps in times past, danced on the embers and more recently were cooked directly on the oven top.

The island teems with wild rabbits and boiled rabbit is an old favourite. You can sample even older cooking during the annual Middle Ages Week in the island's capital, Visby, in mid-August. You're transported to 1361, with those around you dressed accordingly and playing music of that age. You can sip *gotlandsdricku*, mediaeval mead based on hops and juniper. Even older is food made from *spelt*, Sweden's ancient cereal grain. It was cultivated in the Stone Age but disappeared during the Viking Age (800–1050 A.D.), except on Gotland, and is now making a comeback with foodies throughout Sweden. A real survivor.

Fishing has always been vital for Öland and Gotland and, just as with lamb, the islands compete for the best flounder dishes. On both islands, the little flat fish is often served smoked. So which island's is better? Look at it from another angle: serve me and my friends freshly smoked fish and add a superb sunset: if it's on Öland, their fish wins, if it's on Gotland, they get the nod. But of course on Gotland you're likely to get saffron pudding with dewberry preserve for dessert...

Hopping back to the mainland, we continue westward through Småland to the next province, Västergötland, the "birthplace" of the potato in Sweden — it was here that agriculture and industry pioneer Jonas Alströmer in 1724 poked into Swedish soil the first of what would become Sweden's vegetable staple. Potatoes

Klimpinge in Skegrie, Skåne.

had in fact been grown in Sweden before, when scientist and writer Olof Rudbeck the Elder cultivated them in the university city of Uppsala — but only for their pretty flowers. It never struck him that they could be dug up, boiled and served with dill for dinner.

The wide and fertile Västgöta Plain, covering a quarter of the province's area, dominates the landscape between the great lakes of Vänern and Vättern. Conditions are ideal for agriculture, cattle-raising and dairy farming. Some of the milk is processed in the city of Falköping, making marvellous matured cheeses. There is a trade fair for cheese-makers in the city of Skara every September, attracting producers from throughout the country. You might be offered *potkäs*, a fine local product. Country households used to save bits of cheese, often scraps, in a jar. When visitors were due, cream and spices were mixed in. If the visitors were VIPs a dash of brandy would be added. Today it's available in shops, sold in dainty small pots. It adds a special touch to any cheese tray.

Västergötland is also the home of *grynkorv*, a local sausage, best eaten with potato puree. Despite the many good fishing lakes, traditional dishes are often meat-based: sausage, brawn (head cheese) and roasts. The meat can equally be from tame animals as from wild — elks (moose) roam the forests near Halleberg and Hunneberg.

One or two elks probably find their way across the province border to Dalsland, that cross-section of culinary Sweden, where there's almost everything. The old tradition of farm outposts was slow to die out in northern Dalsland; there are rivers and lakes aplenty for anglers; crayfish are tucked away in the lakes; there's room in the forests for game, mushrooms and berries; and in the south fertile plains stretch out under farms and grazing cattle. When the cows calve, the first fat milk is collected for *kalvdans* ("calf dance"), a smooth, thin pudding eaten hot or cold. It used to be common throughout Dalsland province and in many other dairy-farming districts in Sweden.

Dalsland is a small province but boasts Sweden's only boat bridge: the Håverud aquaduct. It straddles a ravine and rapids and is part of the Dalsland Canal. It was a sensation when inaugurated in 1860 and remains a classic "Kodak moment".

At Lake Vättern, we hop on a boat to take another canal back east, the Göta Canal, linking Sweden's east and west coasts. Passing several locks, we glide through Östergötland. The canal took 22 years to build with the help of 58,000 men, and was already obsolete as transport infrastructure when inaugurated in 1832. It is far more popular as a modern tourist experience.

The Östgöta Plain is ancient farming land and wheat has been grown there for centuries. One city is fittingly called "flourtown" — Mjölby. The town still supplies much of Sweden with flour, and pancakes and puddings have long been table staples here. Some claim that Sweden's beloved yellow pea soup comes from Östergötland; peas are widely grown here as well as white cabbage for old-fashioned soup with boiled pork. It was no coincidence that two of Sweden's oldest monasteries, Alvastra and Vreta, were founded close to the richest soil since the monks and the nuns contributed to culinary progress. A true dinner-table classic, *slottstek* ("castle roast", similar to beef à la mode), may be from here. Its traditional sauce is flavoured with tomato, vinegar, syrup and marinated sprat. The modern custom, however, is to serve the meat with a cream sauce and savoury jelly.

To the west is Lake Vättern with its fresh-water fish, to the east, the Baltic with herring fished off Bråviken, and to the north there's Kolmården with its exotic animal reserve and game in the forests. The province has one of Sweden's oldest glassworks at Reijmyre, founded in 1810. We choose a pair of hand-made *snaps* glasses and toast the company in the local specialty, Östgöta Sädes, one of the few spiced snaps distilled from grain, not potato. It is currently produced by the state-owned liquor maker Vin&Sprit in a distant province.

Refreshed, we proceed north, arriving in Södermanland province. We stay with beverages, since much of the barley that is the province's biggest grain crop goes to beer brewing, and a large one with a nice head seems to fit. And what better place to order it than at Nyköpingshus, the castle of a famous 14th-century banquet? (King Birger, lusting for revenge against his brothers Erik and Valdemar, lured them to a feast in 1317, then starved them to death in the tower. These days, the comme-morative banquet is far more peace-oriented, with concerts and theatre.)

Undulating fields and meadows cover the landscape, broken up by a splatter of lakes, often with a manor house or a farmstead not far from the water's edge. This is where the Stockholm aristocracy built their imposing country-seats; typical is the manor house at Julita, close to Katrineholm, now open to the public. The manors often had small apple orchards. The harvested fruit went to the farm's *statare*, the poor labourers who ran the farm for a pittance in wages plus accommodation. Their struggling existence has been famously chronicled by writer Ivar Lo Johansson, himself brought up in a *statare* family.

On Södermanland's coast, diet naturally centred on what the sea provided in the way of Baltic herring and other fish, while the inland dined on potato pudding or the province's flagship dish, *korngrynskaka* (barley pudding) served with pan-fried salted pork and lingonberry preserve. Farmers often ate *ölsupa*, a strong consommé mixed with beer, usually accompanied by eggs and bread.

We take the train north from Södertälje. One of the city's specialties is a kind of pretzel, *kringla*, you used to be able to buy at the station. Travelling over field and farm and skirting Stockholm, our next stop is in Uppland province. We step off in the city of Uppsala, once the site of heathen sacrificial rituals finally halted by the missionary Ansgar, and now a dignified university city.

Carl Linnaeus, the pioneering botanist, may have been born in Småland province but it was in Uppsala that he worked on his ingenious system of classifying plants and animals. His home in Hammarby, with its variety of plants and herbs, is worth a visit.

The Uppsala Plain, one of Sweden's largest agricultural providers, grows oats, barley, wheat and rapeseed. Broad beans also grow in the province and *bönvälling* (bean gruel) used to be popular. The beans and milk are boiled into a delightfully mild soup. *Rotvälska* is a Swedish word expression roughly corresponding to "gobbledygook" or unintelligible speech, but is also the name of an Uppland stew containing swede (rutabaga), carrot, potato and salt-cured pork. The stew must be thick enough to eat with a knife and fork. The province produces dillweed, chives and parsley and farmers around the city of Enköping once had a reputation for the best horseradish. Rye grain goes to the still-famous *Uppsalakubben* (Uppsala block bread), its dough boiled in huge drums to make a heavy, moist loaf.

In the large mansions around Lake Mälaren, cost was thrown to the winds where food was concerned. If oysters were desired, horses were sent dashing to the west coast and back; if wine was wished for, there was burgundy from France or Rhine wines from Germany. Life was considerably harder for the mill workers in the north of the province and farm holdings along the coast were small, making the farmers of the Roslagen region dependent on fishing as a side income. Fish was often stewed and perch stew remains a delicacy. These days, much of Roslagen is a summer holiday destination, especially for Stockholmers.

As soon as schools close for summer, holidaymakers arrive and the countless former farming cottages give welcome respite from the grind of the city. Where once famine inched close to farmhouses, beautifully kept cottages provide a few weeks' rest and the joy of washing in an enamel basin and using an outhouse.

It is a wonderful place to be at Midsummer. This heathen celebration of light has weathered years of Lutheran restraint. Swedes continue to dress the maypole with twigs and leaves and plait flowered wreathes for each other's hair. Even today, oungsters can be seen wandering over meadows in search of the traditional seven kinds of flowers to put under their pillows, to dream of a coming love.

Gettlinge gravefield on the island of Öland.

Coffee time

Typically, a Swedish *kaffekalas* (literally: coffee party) should offer seven different kinds of cookies, as well as buns, sponge cake and ideally a cake with whipped-cream topping as the crowning glory. But even in the old days it was impossible to finish everything. A little paper bag was often placed beside the coffee cup to allow guests to take home what was over. We've chosen three favourites. Cool on a grate and store in airtight jars. Can be deep-frozen.

Oatmeal cookies
Makes about 30

75 g butter
1 dl porridge oats
1 dl white flour
1 dl caster sugar

2 tbsp cream
2 tbsp dark syrup
1/2 tsp baking powder

Warm the oven to 200C/400F/GM6. Melt the butter in a saucepan and mix in the other ingredients to make a smooth batter. Drop a tablespoonful at a time onto a baking tray covered with greaseproof paper. Keep the cookies apart, as they expand. Bake in the middle of the oven about 5 minutes until brown.

Dreams
Makes about 50

100 g butter
3 dl caster sugar, 2 tsp vanilla sugar
1 dl cooking oil, e.g. rapeseed

1 tsp hartshorn/US: Baker's Ammonia (ammonium carbonate)
about 5 dl white flour

Warm the oven to 150C/300F/GM2. Beat the butter, sugar and vanilla sugar until smooth, drizzling in the oil. Mix the hartshorn/Baker's Ammonia with a little flour and blend in. Work in the rest of the flour.
Roll the dough into two chubby snakes. Cut each into about 25 pieces and roll into balls. Arrange them on greaseproof paper on baking trays. Bake in the middle of the oven about 20 minutes until dry but before they brown.

Farmer cakes
Makes about 70

200 g butter
2 dl caster sugar
1 tbsp dark syrup
5 1/2 dl white flour

1 dl almonds, coarsely chopped
1 tsp bicarbonate of soda
1 tbsp water

Warm the oven to 200C/400F/GM6. Beat the butter, sugar and syrup until porous. Mix in the flour and the unpeeled, coarsely chopped almonds. Dissolve the bicarbonate of soda in water and mix in. Roll the dough into snakes about three fingers thick. Store in the fridge half an hour. Cut into fingernail-thick slices and arrange on a greased baking tray. Bake near the top of the oven for 8–10 minutes.

Cinnamon rolls

October 4 is Cinnamon Roll Day (*kanelbullens dag*) in Sweden. Rolls are baked by schoolchildren and bakeries work at high-stress. The cinnamon bun is by a mile Sweden's bun of choice. In the early 1400s, the Spaniards and Portuguese scoured the world for spices (amongst other treasures). And when Sweden's East India Company was founded in Gothenburg in 1731, spices were a major cargo.

Makes about 40 rolls

150 g butter
5 dl milk
50 g fresh yeast (approx. 25 g dried)
1 1/2 dl caster sugar
1 tsp salt
1 tsp crushed cardamom seeds
about 15 dl white flour
40 muffin cases, lowline

Filling

150 g butter
2 1/4 dl caster sugar
1 dl cinnamon

Glaze

1 egg
granulated sugar

Melt the butter in a saucepan, add the milk and warm to 37C/99F. Crumble the yeast into a bowl. Add the milk mixture, absorbing the yeast. Add sugar, salt and the cardamom. Mix in the flour a little at a time, saving 1 dl. Knead the dough until it is smooth and detaches from the sides of the bowl (about 10–12 min.). Cover and leave to rise for about 30 minutes.

Beat the butter, sugar and cinnamon until smooth. Arrange the muffin cases on baking trays. Set the oven to 225C/450F/GM8.

Empty the dough onto a baking board (with your saved 1 dl flour) and divide in half. Roll out each into a rectangle. Spread filling on one half of the rectangle. Gently press the other half over, then cut into about 20 strips. Twist each strip and knot it. Put the knots into the muffin cases. Cover with a cloth and let rise for about 20 minutes.

Glaze the buns with beaten egg and sprinkle with granulated sugar. Bake in the middle of the oven for about 10 minutes. Cover the buns and let cool on a grate.

Strawberry layer cake

This cake is a Swedish midsummer classic. The layers can be put together in advance, leaving the decoration for the last minute. Vary using raspberries or other berries. Homemade custard is obviously yummiest, but there are decent store-bought kinds. Serves 10–12.

Cake base

4 eggs	1 dl potato flour
2 dl caster sugar	2 tsp baking powder
1 dl white flour	breadcrumbs for the dish

Filling and decoration

3 dl custard	1 litre strawberries
1 dl orange juice	6 dl whipping cream
2 dl strawberry or raspberry jam	a few lemon balm leaves (optional)

Heat the oven to 175C/350F/GM4. Grease a round springform pan and coat with breadcrumbs. Beat the eggs and sugar fluffy. Mix the flours and baking powder, then fold into the egg/sugar mixture.

Pour the mixture into the pan and bake on the lowest rung for approx. 40 minutes. Poke a matchstick or a spit into the cake; when it comes out clean, the cake is ready. Let the pan cool a bit before loosening the cake. Then cover and let the cake cool completely on a grate.

Cut the cake into three layers. Place the bottom one on a cake-doily on a dish. Moisten with a little orange juice and spread with jam. Attach the next layer. Moisten with the juice and spread with custard. Place the last layer on top and moisten with juice.

Whip the cream. Spread on and around the cake, saving a little. Decorate with strawberry halves and if you like, a few lemon balm leaves. Pipe the last cream around the edges. A great companion for coffee or cordial.

Vanilla custard

2 dl milk	1 1/2 vanilla pods
1 + 2 dl heavy cream	3 egg yolks
2 tbsp cornstarch + 1 tbsp water	2 tbsp caster sugar

Boil up the milk, 1 dl of the cream and the cornstarch dissolved in water. Add the vanilla seeds and the scraped pods. Bring back to the boil, remove from the heat. Extract the vanilla pods.

Whisk the yolks and sugar, then fold into the milk mixture. Simmer gently while stirring. If boiled, the custard will curdle. When it begins to thicken, remove from the heat, strain and let cool. When the custard is quite cool, whip up the remaining cream and fold in.

Ginger biscuits

Christmas ain't Christmas in Sweden without ginger biscuits! Originally, they were medicinal and far spicier. In the Middle Ages, they were said to cure sicknesses, cholera included. The biscuits were also renowned as sexual stimulants and allegedly cured depression. This reputation survives in the traditional ginger-biscuit invitation: "They'll make you nice!" There's no longer pepper in *pepparkakor*, but the dough is richly pungent with other spices. Roll out straight onto greaseproof paper to get the dough extra thin. The dough will keep for weeks in the refrigerator.

Makes about 100 biscuits

100 g butter
2 3/4 dl (200 g) brown sugar
1 dl dark syrup
1 dl cream
2 tsp ground ginger
2 tsp ground cinnamon
2 tsp ground cloves
about 8 1/2 dl white flour
2 tsp bicarbonate of soda

Mix butter, sugar and syrup until smooth. Add cream and spices. Mix the bicarbonate of soda into the flour, then mix everything into a dough. Wrap in plastic wrap and store overnight in the fridge.

Warm oven to 225C/450F/GM8. Roll out the dough thinly on greaseproof paper and stencil out shapes. Transfer paper to baking trays and bake in the middle of the oven about 5 minutes. Keep a close watch — they should be dark brown but not burnt. Let cool on a grate. Store airtight.

Lenten buns

Every Swede's favourite guilty bun can be eaten with a spoon from a deep dish where it sits in a moat of warm milk. Or just wolf it down. Lent used to mean 40 days of meagre diet, and it was common to "fill up" before the fasting started. Fasting is a distant memory for most of us so *semlor* have become a delicacy enjoyed in the run-up to Easter. The modern variety has whipped cream in a cavity topped by a piece of the bun. Diced, candied orange peel is a delicious addition to the filling.

Makes 12-15 buns

100 g butter
3 dl milk
50 g fresh yeast (approx. 25 g dried)
1/2 tsp salt
1 dl caster sugar
1 egg
1/2 tsp hartshorn/US: Baker's Ammonia (ammonium carbonate)
slightly less than 1 l flour

Filling and decoration

150 g almond paste
2 dl whipped cream
icing sugar

Melt the butter and add the milk. Heat carefully to a tepid 37C/99F. Crumble the yeast into a big bowl and dissolve it with a little of the milk mixture. Add salt, sugar, the rest of the milk mixture and the egg.
Mix the hartshorn/Baker's Ammonia with a little of the flour. Mix in more flour gradually. Knead the dough by hand 10–12 minutes until smooth and shiny. Cover and leave to rise 30 minutes.
Heat the oven to 250C/480F/GM9. Tip the dough onto a work surface and knead again. Make into balls about the size of a small orange. Arrange them on oven paper on a baking sheet and let rise covered another 20–30 minutes. Glaze with beaten egg and bake in the middle of the oven for 8–10 minutes. Let cool on a grate under a cloth.
Cut and save a shallow circle in the top of each bun and scoop out some of the bread, mixing it with the coarsely grated almond paste. You might want to moisten with a little cream. Stuff the buns with the filling and pipe whipped cream over. Cut your saved circle into a triangle and put it on the top. Sprinkle with icing sugar.

Swedish raspberry fool

This can be a dessert, a snack, breakfast or just a treat. Raspberry fool is soul food for Swedes, evoking those special childhood memories. You can vary the fruit, substituting blueberries or sliced strawberries. See that you don't boil the berries, or they lose their flavour.

Serves 4

500 ml (250 g) fresh or deep-frozen raspberries
2 dl red cordial concentrate
4 dl water
3 tbsp potato starch or cornstarch

Serve with

milk

Put the raspberries in a bowl. Mix the cordial, water and potato starch in a saucepan. Whisk over heat until it boils, thickening the mixture. Pour over the raspberries and blend. Serve lukewarm or cold with milk.

Rosehip soup with macaroons

If instant rosehip soup is the only kind you've had, one of life's seminal delicacies awaits you. Fresh is totally not the same as readymade! Fresher, healthier and stuffed with vitamins. If you can't find fresh rosehips, health-food shops have dried rosehips which you soak for 24 hours before using. Home-made macaroons are easy to make and are delicious and delightfully chewy.

Serves 4

6–7 dl fresh or soaked rosehips
2 litres water
1–1 1/2 dl caster sugar
1 tbsp potato starch or cornstarch
1/2 dl orange juice concentrate

Serve with

macaroons
whipped cream
vanilla icecream

Rinse the rosehips. Boil the water, put the rosehips in and boil them until soft. Press through a strainer. You'll need about 1 litre so add more water if necessary.
Return the mash to a saucepan. Mix in the potato starch and simmer while whisking. Add the orange juice and sweeten to taste. Serve cold with ice cream, whipped cream and macaroons.

Macaroons

100 g almonds
water for blanching
1 egg white
13/4 dl icing sugar

Heat the oven to 150C/300F/GM2.
Blanch the almonds in boiling water. Rinse after about a minute, then pull off the skins and grind the blanched almonds or put in a blender until finely chopped. Mix the almonds and icing sugar.
Beat the egg white vigorously and fold in the almond-sugar mix. Transfer the batter to a piping bag and pipe small peaks onto the oven paper. Bake in the middle of the oven about 20 minutes. Store airtight.

Swedish cheesecake pudding with cloudberry jam

No Swedish cheesecake pudding at the party? Then it's no party. That's the way it used to be in Småland province. At the mission church jumble sale or auction, the good matrons of the congregation would check out each other's cheesecakes. They had to be high and moist-but-not-too-moist. Serve with cloudberry preserve or your own favourite jam. You can deep-freeze the surplus whey for the next time you bake bread.

Serves 8

3 litres standard milk (3%)
1/2 dl white flour
1/2 tbsp extract of rennet (available at pharmacies)
1 tbsp water
50 g blanched and peeled almonds
3/4 dl icing sugar
2 eggs
2 dl crème fraîche or sour cream

Serve with

cloudberry preserve or other jam
whipped cream

Pour a little of the milk into the flour and mix. Heat the rest of the milk to exactly 35C/95F. Mix the cheese rennet and water, and, stirring continuously, add the flour mix and cheese rennet to the milk, removing from the heat. Cover and leave for 30–40 minutes. With a knife, cut into the cheese that will have formed and release the whey. Press the cheese through a sieve and let it drain properly.
Chop the almonds coarsely and mix with the icing sugar. Whisk the egg and blend with the crème fraîche or sour cream. Mix everything with the cheese. Heat the oven to 175C/350F/GM4. Grease a medium dish (about 2 litres/4 pints), fill it with the cheese mixture and bake for about 90 minutes, until the surface is golden brown. Don't touch the cake during baking. Serve while still slightly warm with cloudberry preserve or jam and whipped cream.

Cloudberry preserve

500 g cloudberries
3/4–1 dl caster sugar

Layer cloudberries and sugar in a bowl. Store cold overnight to separate the juice. Stir once in a while before going to bed.

Pancakes with bilberry/blueberry jam

The first written Swedish record of pancakes is from 1538. What they looked like then is anybody's guess. The advantages of small over large pancakes: easier to make, perfect for outings, and you can eat a lot! Swedes have dedicated iron pans with round depressions but an ordinary frypan will do. Your pancakes might not be perfectly shaped but they'll taste just as great. Vary using raspberry or strawberry preserve.

Serves 6

3 eggs
1 1/2 dl cold water
1 tsp caster sugar
a pinch of salt
1 1/2 dl white flour
1 1/2 dl milk
1 dl heavy cream
2–3 tbsp butter

Serve with

blueberry preserve
whipped cream

Whisk the eggs and water and add, little by little, sugar, salt and flour. Mix in milk and cream. Let the batter swell for 10 minutes.
Melt the butter in a small saucepan and brush the pan for the first batch. Pour the remaining butter into the batter. Fry thin cakes of about cup size. Serve with preserves and whipped cream.

Blueberry preserve

1/2 litre blueberries
1 tbsp water
1 1/2 dl caster sugar

Boil the blueberries and water for about 5 minutes, adding sugar a little at a time. Pour into a hot jar and seal immediately. Store cool.

Rhubarb crumble

The first part of the word "rhubarb" is said to come from the old Greek word for the River Volga, "Rha", where it grew and the second part from "barbarian" because the plant came from the wild countries beyond the Black Sea. The first printed recipe in Swedish dates from 1884 so this is a dessert with a pedigree. For best flavour, harvest while the stalks are still slim and young. Cut them into fingernail-size pieces. (If you've got a lot, deep-freeze some for year-round use.) This crumble can be made with other berries and fruit: blueberries, apples, raspberries, etc.

Serves 8	500 g rhubarb
	1 dl caster sugar
	1 msk cornstarch
	butter for the dish

Crumble dough	100 g butter
	3 dl white flour
	3/4 dl caster sugar

Serve with	whipped cream or vanilla sauce

Heat oven to 225C/450F/GM8. Chop the butter into small dice and pinch into the flour until you get crumbs. De-string the rhubarb, cut it into small sections and mix with the sugar and cornstarch.
Grease a pie dish with butter and tip the rhubarb mix in. Spread the crumble over and bake the dish low in the oven for about 25 minutes or until golden brown. Serve with whipped cream or vanilla sauce.

Rice porridge

The first record of rice porridge in Sweden is 1328, at the funeral wake for the father of St. Bridget of Sweden (1303–1373). In the 1700s, rice porridge was served at all the finest farmhouse parties. It can be served at any time of year, but it's a definite must after the Swedish Christmas smorgasbord. Traditional families still set aside a plate for the elf who sneaks in before dawn on Christmas Eve. Hide an almond in the porridge and whoever gets it gets a task, like composing a thank-you in rhyme to the hostess. In the old days, if a single young man or woman found the nut, it was a sign that the coming year would bring true love.

Serves 4

1 1/2 dl pudding/short-grain rice
3 dl water
3/4 tsp salt
6–7 dl milk
1 cinnamon stick
1 tsp caster sugar
1 tbsp butter

Serve with

cold milk
ground cinnamon
one almond
sugar optional

Boil rice, water and salt. Let boil quietly under cover for 10 minutes. Add milk and the cinnamon stick and stir well. Cover again and let the porridge swell for 30 minutes at very low heat. Don't uncover or stir. Remove from the heat and leave for another 10 minutes. Then add the sugar and butter. Hide an almond in the porridge. Serve with cold milk and ground cinnamon.

Rice à la Malta

Should Rice à la Malta include orange segments in the rice? Should it be served with cordial sauce? There are opposing factions, but we'll side with the latter. (But next time, add skinned orange segments, just before serving — in too long, they become bitter.) Garnish with roasted almond slivers.

Serves 4

approx. 5 dl rice porridge (see recipe)
1 1/2 dl whipping cream
1 tbsp caster sugar
1–2 tsp vanilla sugar

Cordial sauce

2 dl red cordial, e.g. raspberry concentrate
3 dl water
1 1/2 tbsp potato starch or cornstarch

See that the rice porridge has been cooled in the fridge. Whip the cream and fold it into the pudding. Sweeten with sugar and vanilla sugar.
Mix the cordial and water. Whisk in the potato starch, bring to the boil and whisk until the sauce thickens. Let it cool in the fridge. Serve the rice and cordial sauce for dessert.

Saffron pudding

As with rice, the first mention of saffron in Swedish came at the wake for St. Bridget's father in 1328. Saffron became especially popular on the island of Gotland, used in a pudding. The delicacy gained a foothold on the mainland. It's served year-round. The classic accompaniment is preserve made from the dewberries (*Rubus caesius*) that grow wild on Gotland. But blackberry or raspberry does just fine.

Serves 6-8

1 batch rice porridge (see recipe)
3 eggs
1–2 saffron sachets (0.5–1 g)
1 tbsp caster sugar
1 dl raisins
a large pinch of coarsely ground cardamom seeds
1 dl finely chopped almonds

Serve with

fruit preserve
whipped cream

Prepare the rice porridge from the recipe. Heat the oven to 200C/400F/GM6. Whisk the eggs. Pound the saffron and sugar in a mortar. Mix the saffron and eggs and fold into the pudding with the cardamom, raisins and almonds.
Grease an ovenproof dish of about 2 litres/4 pints, spread out the mixture and bake for about 30 minutes until the pudding has sct and the surface has a bit of colour. Serve with your favourite fruit preserve and whipped cream.

Baked apples with vanilla sauce

Another dessert guaranteed to spark nostalgia! In Sweden, Skåne province has the most famous apples but there are fine varieties almost throughout the country. Choose a soft variety. Prepare the dish before dinner — it's best if baked just before serving. A special apple-coring tool helps but it's not hard to cut the cores out using a thin, sharp knife.

Serves 4

4 apples
100 g grated or crumbled almond paste
1–2 tsp cinnamon
50 g butter

Heat the oven to 200C/400F/GM6. Peel and core the apples. Grease an oven dish with a little of the butter. Mix the rest of the butter with the almond paste and the cinnamon. Place the apples in the dish and fill the core crevice with the mixture. Bake for about 20 minutes. Serve warm with vanilla sauce.

Vanilla sauce

2 dl milk
1 + 2 dl whipping cream
1 1/2 vanilla pod
3 egg yolks
2 tbsp caster sugar

Boil the milk and 1 dl of the cream with the vanilla seeds. Put in the scraped vanilla pod as well. Bring back to the boil, then remove from the heat. Remove the pod.
Whisk the egg yolks and sugar and stir them into the milk mixture. Heat to just under boiling point, stirring all the time. (If boiled, the custard will curdle.) When it begins to thicken, take it off the heat, strain and cool. Just before serving, whip the remaining 2 dl of cream and fold in.

Kitchen shortcuts

In the old days, kitchen tips and shortcuts were passed down from one generation to another. You inherited wisdom without thinking, everything from smart tools to cunning tips. Then suddenly it's your turn to send forward.

Corkscrew

Invaluable when boiling a head of cabbage for cabbage dolmas, for example. Screw it into the thick root and you've got a handle for lifting the cabbage out gently. As the cabbage softens, lift it out and pull off the soft leaves. Then lower it back.

Virgins at the table

In the old days, Swedish restaurants used to serve snaps and sweet, sticky *punsch* liqueur in little individual carafes. The carafe was called a "virgin" and held enough spirits (8.2 cl/2.5 fl.oz) for one guest. The carafe was in a glass bowl filled with ice or, for *punsch*, hot water. It's a fun custom. Shop around for nice little bottles to chill your snaps when serving herring and warm the *punsch* for the pea soup.

Bay leaves

These shiny, green aromatic leaves (*Laurus nobilis*) have strong associations in Greek mythology and are used in both Greek and Swedish home cooking for their good flavour. When the sun god Apollo fell in love with beautiful Daphne, her father turned her into a laurel tree to protect her virginity. We don't often remember that when we're adding spices to *kalops*.

Drying wild mushrooms

Dry your chanterelles or cep and they'll keep really well. Spread out the wild mushrooms (more accurately: fungi) on oven paper and dry (50C/125F) overnight or until dry enough to crumble when rubbed. Keep in sealed jars. Hydrate a half-hour before using. Tastes like fresh.

Rose hips

International cooking dictionaries mention rose hips only in connection with making eau de vie and confectionary. That's leaving out the true delight: rose hip soup! Pick the fruit when they're deep orange-red, pull apart and scrape out the dry fruitlets. If you don't want to make soup immediately, dry the fruit as for wild mushrooms or simply freeze.

Griddles

The best frying pan is indubitably the one your grandmother "ran in" before you were even a glint in your father's eye. Well looked-after (clean with water only, never detergent) it is indestructible. A cast-iron pancake griddle is also perfect for frying eggs and hamburgers. Swedish frypans and pots in cast-iron, from Skeppshult and other makers, are the best you'll find.

Herring

Coating herring with egg and breadcrumbs preserves its flavour. For best results, do it twice: turn the fish in plain flour, then dip into beaten egg, then turn again in stoneground rye flour or breadcrumbs. For Baltic herring, it's popular to press two fillets together with chopped dill and/or caviar in the middle. Then follow the above procedure and fry in butter.

Ginger biscuits

Christmas isn't Christmas without crispy ginger biscuits! It's easiest to roll them, really thin, straight onto oven paper. See that the dough is refrigerator-cold; you can also chill the rolling pin a few minutes. A straight bottle works if you don't have a rolling pin. Stencil out the biscuits with a glass or cut out with a knife. Bake, then cool on a grate and store in sealed jars.

Rolling pins

When rolling out dough for crispbread, begin with a regular rolling pin. Roll the round breads really thin, dusting generously with flour. Finish up with the jagged *kruskavel* (approx. "Roller Docker") or just prick with a fork. This is to prevent the bread blistering in the oven. Roll directly onto oven paper and use pre-warmed baking trays and you'll get the very best crispbread.

Bread

Get out all ingredients except the yeast so everything is at room temperature when you begin. If your kitchen is cold, kick-start the rising process by warming the flour in a microwave for a minute before mixing with the yeast and liquid. While the dough is rising, cover the bowl with clingwrap or a lid. The more moist the dough surface is, the better the bread.

Cordial

When making cordial clean bottles are really important. Save your empty liquor bottles — they're the cleanest. Friends and neighbours will give you theirs. For wine and other bottles, do a final rinse with a splash of liquor. Wash corks with liquor too. This lets you store cordial without preservatives. You can freeze it in half-filled plastic bottles.

Sweden's 25 provinces

Milieu and tableware

SVARTSÖ HERRGÅRDSPENSIONAT, SVARTSÖ

SVENSKT TENN

K2 KERAMIK
Helena Hättestrand
Tina Lundberg
Ulrika Ahlsten
Anna Schröder
Greta Stelling

G.A.D
Mona Malmström
Ingegerd Råman
Ingela Karlsson
Anna Rutz

GUSTAVSBERGS PORSLINSFABRIK
Signe Persson-Melin
Catharina Kippel
Anette Olsen-Ulmér
Siv Juhlin
Maria Johansson

MIKAELA WILLERS
Cecilia Boström
Krut Studioglas
Elisabeth Ottebring
Karin Eriksson
Charlotta Klingström

BIRGITTA WATZ

BORÅS COTTON
Tina Steijer
Ann-Cathrine Sigrid
Göta Trägårdh

KONSTHANTVERKARNA
Helena Kaiser
Helena Gibson
Richard Rackham
Calle Forsberg
Frida Runnqvist
Karin Bengtsson
Jussi Ojala
Jonas Lindholm
Mårten Medbo
Barbro Johansson
Anna Lerinder
Åsa Jungnelius
Kina Björklund

Reference literature

Det goda Sverige,
Inger Grimlund och Björn Halling,
Page One Publishing
Mathistorisk uppslagsbok,
Jan-Öjvind Swahn,
Ordalaget bokförlag
Sverige – ljus och landskap,
Tore Hagman, Tommy Hammarström
and Per Wästberg,
Bokförlaget Max Ström
Våra högtider,
anthology, Prisma
Vägarnas Bästa 2004–2005,
Mikael Mölstad,
Millhouse förlag

Page 150: Valle, Västergötland.
Page 158: The lighthouse of Närsholmen, on the island of Gotland.

Recipe register

Weights and measures

1 ml = 1 pinch
5 ml = 1 teaspoon (tsp)
15 ml = 1 tablespoon (tbsp)
1 dl (100 ml) = ½ cup
1 litre (1,000 ml) = 5 cups, 40 fluid oz. (fl.oz.)

1 cup = 2.37 dl

50 g = 1.75 oz.
100 g = 3.5 oz.
1 kg (kilo) =1,000 g = 2.2 pounds (lb.)

10 cm = 4 inches
25 cm = 10 inches

1 inch = 2.5 cm

Behind the book

Annica Triberg is well known in food and cooking circles from her work in Gourmet magazine and various television cooking shows. She has published about 30 books, many of them on food.

Per Ranung is a versatile photographer specialising in beautiful interiors from around the world. He is also a skilled photographer of food with a rare feeling for the atmosphere in his images.

Lena Salomonsson is a chef based in the Stockholm archipelago with a solid knowledge of her craft after years spent in the kitchens of renowned Swedish restaurants. She cherishes the seasons' changing ingredients and the treasure of Sweden's traditional recipes.

Tore Hagman is one of Sweden's most prominent nature photographers. He has contributed to several acclaimed books and his pictures communicate an exceptional love for Sweden's landscapes, from the outer archipelago islands to the smallest tuft of grass.